PEACEFUL RESISTANCE

Peaceful Resistance

Building a Palestinian University under Occupation

Gabi Baramki

Foreword by Jimmy Carter

PlutoPress
www.plutobooks.com

First published 2010 by Pluto Press
345 Archway Road, London N6 5AA and
175 Fifth Avenue, New York, NY 10010

Distributed in the United States of America exclusively by
Palgrave Macmillan, a division of St. Martin's Press LLC,
175 Fifth Avenue, New York, NY 10010

www.plutobooks.com

British Library Cataloguing in Publication Data
A catalogue record for this book is available from the British Library

ISBN   978 0 7453 2932 1   Hardback
ISBN   978 0 7453 2931 4   Paperback

Library of Congress Cataloging in Publication Data applied for
10070518 76 A
This book is printed on paper suitable for recycling and made from fully
managed and sustained forest sources. Logging, pulping and manufacturing processes are expected to conform to the environmental standards of
the country of origin. The paper may contain up to 70% post consumer
waste.

10 9 8 7 6 5 4 3 2 1
Designed and produced for Pluto Press by
Curran Publishing Services, Norwich

Printed and bound in the European Union by
CPI Antony Rowe, Chippenham and Eastbourne

CONTENTS

ACKNOWLEDGEMENTS

In writing a personal story of an institution that spans over 70 years of my lifetime, the job of acknowledging the people who influenced me during this period becomes enormous. To try to name them all would be an arduous task and I might still end up omitting some of them in error. But some names and institutions have been so prominent in my life that I have no difficulty remembering them, and no hesitation in thanking them for all they have meant to me.

I start with a general acknowledgement: first to the Birzeit University community, starting with Musa Nasir and his family, and then to my colleagues over the years and my students, some of whom later became colleagues. I learnt a lot from all of them and I thank them for what I am today.

Musa Nasir himself, with whom I first started to work at Birzeit, was a tremendous resource from whom I learned the basic elements of administration and politics. Hanna Nasir was my long time partner with whom I shared the dreams and worries of Birzeit throughout the period from 1959 to the present.

Then there are the few colleagues out of the many who have helped me over the years who became deeply involved in the team that shared the tasks of planning and administration, and helped me in dealing with the daily relations with the Military government, faculty and staff unions, and students, in their capacity as long term members of the University Council: Ramzi Rihan, George Giacaman, Mohammad Hallaj, Sami Sayrafi, Munir Fasheh, Hanan Ashrawi, and Nabeel Kassis, as well as the three Vice Presidents who are no longer with us: Othman Abu Libdeh, Izzat Ghourani and Abdel Latif Barghouti.

Birzeit was blessed with excellent Public Relations officers who were very helpful especially at times when the University was engaged in confrontations with the Israeli army or the Military government, which unfortunately occurred often. Mahdi Abdul Hadi was first and he was especially effective when we started the Council for Higher Education. Akram Haniyyeh joined later and in his quiet way was very helpful with external relations until his stay was interrupted by his deportation. Penny Johnson used her skills to the full in documenting the tumultuous events we endured at Birzeit, from student demonstrations to confrontations with the soldiers, as well as writing press releases and presentations to the general public, the UN, and foreign embassies when the pressure of work did not allow me to do this myself.

My thanks are also due to Albert Aghazarian who, beside doing the work of public relations, was my companion whenever I had meetings with the Military Governor or other officials. Most important was his presence during the difficult times in the middle of conflicts with the authorities when he could diffuse the situation with his Hebrew expressions, turning a heated situation into a comic one.

In writing this book, I must give the credit for Nigel Parry who helped me start it and did at least fourteen recording sessions with me to get the project going. When Nigel left the Public Relations office at Birzeit rather abruptly, some of the tapes that he made were lost and after a salvage operation the work was continued by Elise Aghazarian. Her enthusiasm and perseverance were inspiring and for this I am indeed grateful. I am grateful to Karl Sabbagh for helping to bring this project to completion through his knowledge of the authorial process and his valuable input into the final manuscript. However, this book would not have seen the light without the tireless efforts of my old student and friend Gabriel Alexander Khoury who, not only saw to it that the manuscript was in good hands for editing and publication, but also followed up on all details and management of this project till the finish line. To him I am truly grateful.

Finally, I could not have achieved what I have over the last fifty years without the constant support of my family: my parents who guided me during the formative years of this long journey at Birzeit; and my wife Haifa, who shared with me the particularly difficult events of the Israeli occupation. Adversity has different effects on families, but in our case, it brought us closer to one another. Haifa did a superlative job keeping the family together as we experienced the wars of 1967 and 1973, the anxieties and worry whenever the phone rang at our home in the middle of the night, or when I had to stay for long hours at the University.

Gabi Baramki

FOREWORD

Through my years of work for Middle East peace, I consistently have endorsed education as a way to foster tolerance and understanding of others. I also pray and work for nonviolent means to end the occupation of the West Bank and Gaza. As the oldest university in the occupied territories, Birzeit has been a leader in promoting both. Birzeit also has been at the forefront of efforts to build independent, efficient, national Palestinian institutions, which now are providing a foundation for the creation of a Palestinian state. Birzeit helped foster Palestinian identity, and its student council elections have provided generations of Palestinian leaders with practical experience in democracy – experience very much in evidence during Palestinian elections The Carter Center has monitored. Gabi Baramki's work has made much of this possible. His tireless devotion to Birzeit University has allowed the institution to survive and even thrive against incredible odds.

Many individuals associated with Birzeit, including Haidar Abdul Shafi and Hanan Ashrawi, have played critical roles in efforts to negotiate peace with Israel, especially in the context of the 1991 Madrid Conference and the early years of negotiations among the parties. I also have had the privilege of knowing many Birzeit staff personally throughout the years, including Hanan Ashrawi, Albert Aghazarian, Hanna Nasir, and of course, Gabi Baramki. Their dedication and skill have long been an asset to the Palestinian people.

Birzeit University is a testament to the resourcefulness of a people under military occupation and their desire to build a state of their own. Students and staff demonstrate the intense commitment to education that has long characterized the Palestinian people. But perhaps most importantly, Birzeit illustrates a space where Palestinians of diverse political views coexist, despite their differences. I hope this book will help remind Palestinians—especially the leadership on all sides—of these values that have allowed their community to survive so many hardships, values that are needed now more than ever in the inexorable move toward statehood.

Jimmy Carter
US President 1977–81
Nobel Peace Prize 2002
July 10, 2009

INTRODUCTION

Birzeit University in the Israeli-occupied Palestinian West Bank has been perceived by Israel as a threat. I happen to agree with this analysis but for reasons diametrically opposed to those offered by the Israelis.

Birzeit is not a threat because there are 'guns instead of books on shelves', as Israeli tales would have it, but rather because, as an academic institution and testing ground for ideas, it has become a place that has produced many Palestinian leaders at both international and community level.

As an independent Palestinian institution, Birzeit has been pre-eminent in demonstrating to the world that the Palestinians are a civilised, academic and vibrant people with a distinct national identity and, in common with all human beings, they have their own set of wishes, dreams, hopes and fears.

The real threat that Birzeit poses is not military, terrorist, anti-Semitic or even anti-Israel. The threat that Birzeit poses is that it is a shining example of what the Palestinians can do against incredible odds. Birzeit has been a pioneer in the practice of democracy in Palestine. It has given hope to a people who have been given little reason for hope. It has demonstrated that the human spirit is alive in Palestine, and it has given us a glimpse of what the Palestinians can achieve in the future. If a university subjected to continual harassment by the Israeli state, including its closure by military order for almost five years, can survive, continue to maintain its principles of freedom, respect and dignity, and even flourish, one can only imagine what would happen if it were given the space to grow. The threat is to the Zionist dream of having Palestine – the land – without its people, to 'spirit' the Palestinians out of Palestine as Theodor Herzl suggested. What Birzeit did was to make sure that the people stayed on the land.

Birzeit University is like a well-crafted fishing net that has been filled with a myriad of varieties of fish from the many rivers and streams of Palestinian society. From Birzeit, many have been sent out to feed the hungry, to build the necessary social structures and attend to the needs of a country that has been strangled by almost 40 years of military occupation.

This book is not a political manifesto for the Palestinian people, nor is it a one-sided account of a conflict that many shy away from out of fear of being labelled as 'biased'. Rather, it is an invitation to experience the lives of normal people in a difficult and testing situation that they had little opportunity to avoid.

By the end of this story I do not expect you to hate the Israeli people. Instead I believe that you will be moved by the honesty and reality of the Palestinians who tell their story. In a world where even the simplest of truths are offensive to some, I do not expect everyone to agree with the views expressed in these pages, but I do trust that in the end the reader will understand more about some of the forces that have created the Palestinians' perception of the situation.

This book is not meant to be a comprehensive or final document on the story of Birzeit University, but rather a personal account through the eyes of a few who have given a significant part of their life to build it. It was felt that this would help the book to be, above all else, a good story. I did not wish to write a lifeless history book that would appeal only to those interested in the Middle East, or an academic tome that would end up, unused and dusty, on library bookshelves. It has been written with the intention that anyone can read and relate to the story, whatever their interest.

The story of the university is not complete without going back to the roots, the high school and later on the junior college (see Appendix I, Chronology of Birzeit). Both give the background that led to the university, and both are tied to my life in more ways than by my simply being a student or a teacher and administrator. I became involved in every aspect of the institution: the national, educational, cultural and leadership role, and at various times in its history. I will therefore try to present this part of the story of Birzeit from my first contact as a five-year-old until my retirement from the university, presenting my personal experiences during this long attachment to the institution.

1

GROWING UP IN PALESTINE

I have always loved teaching, though I never set out to establish a career in that field. Birzeit University has enabled me to spend my life helping young people grow into knowledgeable, public-spirited adults, and I cannot think of a more rewarding job. Our students are vastly more numerous and more successful than I ever dared to envisage when the institution launched its first degree course in 1972.

I could not have envisaged, either, the grim reality of running a university under Israeli occupation: the storming of its campus by armed soldiers, the regular imprisonment of students and staff, those long, punitive closures. The wounding, maiming and killing of so many of our students haunts me to this day. Still, we have never given in. Palestinians have the same right to education as young people anywhere and they need that education to build the free, successful society they deserve.

Education was not universally valued among Palestinians when I was young. Only the rich and members of the professional classes expected their children to study. Becoming a nation of refugees, of people living under a destructive, impoverishing military rule, has profoundly changed attitudes. Education is seen as one of very few escape routes. Families scrimp and save, forgoing even the small treats they allow themselves on feast days, to pay for school books and uniforms. Mothers in villages or refugee camps may sell off the few precious pieces of jewellery received as wedding presents so a child can continue into higher education. For the poor, of course, getting an education has never been easy.

My own parents were fortunate. The Baramkis are Palestinian Christians. My father, Andoni Baramki, came from a Greek Orthodox merchant family able to trace back its Jerusalem roots at least 500 years. Although modest in size, Jerusalem had a wealth of inspiring old buildings, such as the multi-layered Church of the Resurrection, the Dome of the Rock with its delicately adorned blue walls, and the Ottoman Citadel now mysteriously known as 'David's Tower'. Moreover, a mini building boom in the 1920s had resulted in box-shaped modern villas springing up alongside traditional Arab houses with double-arched windows, latticed balconies and cupola roofs. So, when my father developed an interest in architecture, his parents sent him to Athens to study the subject at its Fine Arts Academy.

On his return in 1922, my father both designed and built our family home, moving us from the Greek Orthodox section of the Old City to the Sheikh Jarrah quarter outside the Old City wall next to St George's School and Cathedral. Setting up his own company, he built schools, family residences, villas and even churches all over the country. His outstanding work is the graceful Romanian Convent in Jerusalem. My father's style was unique in that it combined the Arabic arch with the Corinthian heads of the columns supporting it. The windows of his designs were lined with rose-red Bethlehem stone, set against white stone from Hebron.

My father became renowned for the quality of his buildings after the earthquake of 1927, when it emerged that every single one of the houses constructed by him had withstood the tremors. This taught me about the value of 'honesty in work' and about 'the need for high quality' – lessons I have tried hard to convey to my students.

What had produced the mini-boom which provided my father with clients was the arrival of the British mandate. By the time I was born in 1929, the Ottoman Empire had collapsed and Palestine was governed by Britain under a League of Nations mandate. This made its inhabitants subjects of King George V, ruled by a British High Commissioner answerable to the British parliament, whose members we could not vote for. However, the League of Nations had bestowed the mandate on Britain only 'until such time as [the inhabitants of Palestine] are able to stand alone'. The League had, in fact, also endorsed 'the establishment in Palestine of a national home for the Jewish people'. This was the beginning of an unfortunate long history of total disregard by the international community of the wishes, opinions and hopes for freedom and self-determination of the great majority of the indigenous Palestinian population, or even recognising their presence as the legal owners of the country. However, since we were the country's indigenous, majority population, most Palestinian Arabs looked forward to eventual national government.

Such a project required an educated population. Palestine was still under-developed, with only one secondary governmental school (the Arab College in Jerusalem). The mandate government had the policy of establishing only a limited number of primary schools in certain rural areas. The two top students from these elementary schools were then transferred to the secondary school in Jerusalem. However there were already primary and secondary schools, some affiliated to religious missions and few national ones, mainly located in Jerusalem, Ramallah, Haifa, Jaffa and Nablus. Middle-class parents from the cities and wealthy families from the villages sent their children, mainly as boarders, to these schools to be educated. When it was time for me to go to the elementary school, my parents decided to send me to Birzeit Higher School, which was established in 1924 by the Nasir family as a national school for boys and girls. It was a modern boarding school with high learning standards.

One of the modern features of the school was that it would be mixed. Palestinian girls tended to be kept at home by all but the most westernized families. Now they would not just be schooled with boys but be taught much the same subjects. Another innovation was that the languages of instruction would be both English and Arabic. Until that point, schools had taught in the mother tongue of their founders, English in the case of Jerusalem's Anglican School, and French if run by the religious order of the Franciscans. While traditional schools taught only in Arabic, those set up by the mandate government hardly bothered with the language. The pupils of the new school would enjoy the blessings of more than one culture.

So, one October morning in 1934 my parents and I set out in the family's bright yellow car to the village of Birzeit, a journey of just over 16 miles from Jerusalem. At that time the road from Jerusalem to Birzeit meandered through Nablus, Ramallah, Ein Sinia and Jifna. It was a narrow road, partially paved until Ein Sinia. It took about an hour by car, which often made me feel car-sick. Once out of Jerusalem, we could enjoy the view of fruit trees and olive groves. Ramallah, a small town at the time, was a summer resort with one hotel, The Ramallah Grand Hotel, commonly known as Hotel Audeh. The town was famous for its delicious grapes, which unfortunately were destroyed by the Phylloxera pest in the early 1950s. From Ramallah we went on the Nablus road as far as Ein Sinia and then took the side road through Jifna village, best known for its 'Mistkawi' apricots. The car struggled to make its way through the unpaved road leading to the village of Birzeit.

Map 1
Birzeit in Palestine,
1920–48

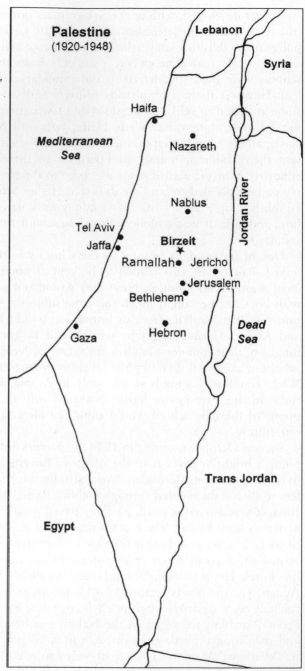

Palestine
(1920-1948)

The school was situated in the home of the Nasir family. Its stern yellow-stone front hid a comfortable, attractive interior made up of tall, spacious rooms with brightly tiled floors. The house was part of a large complex of other thick-walled buildings in the back. A garden whose centre was a giant cypress tree was closed off from the outside by a tall, wrought-iron gate. It was a serene, peaceful spot, which years later would become a battleground between Israeli soldiers and Palestinian students.

My excitement at being in such a new environment was tempered by the shock of being parted from my parents. I was very young. I remember that on my fifth birthday in November, my uncle George, who lived in Germany at the time, came with my parents and brought me a wooden block shaped like a number five with slots for five candles as a birthday present. Being allowed to sleep in the same room as the school's matron, Miss Jaleeleh Aranki, eased my homesickness slightly.

Meeting the other children helped me to settle in. Boarders came from all over Palestine, from cities like Jerusalem, Haifa, Nablus, Gaza and Jaffa, as well as from smaller places such as Tulkarm and Jenin. Some, like me, had arrived alone, others in a group of siblings and cousins. The pupils, boys and girls, came from the country's various Muslim and Christian communities. We were kept busy and encouraged to get on. Were we not all Palestinians? One of the first boys I made friends with was Faruq Najib Nassar, whose father was owner of *Al-Karmel Al-Jadid* newspaper.

Facilities at the new school were fairly basic. The dining room served as a classroom for elementary students, and until the age of eight we were given our baths in small aluminium tubs by women from the village. There was no electricity and the kerosene lamps would be turned off at night. As the school toilets were outside in the courtyard, getting there meant a long, unlit walk away from our second-floor dormitories, often in high winds or rain. Water for toilets and washing was pumped from the cisterns that collected rain from the roof but sometimes ran out in the dry season. Drinking water was brought daily from Birzeit's main spring, called Ein Fleiflch. It arrived at the school in four cans, each 20 litres in capacity, mounted on the back of the school donkey and emptied into fixed a 250-litre container located in the school yard for our use. Throughout my stay at the school, it was the same person, known to the pupils as 'Shurra', who drove the donkey up and down the hill to supply the three buildings with drinking water and pumped the water from the cisterns to the tanks on the roofs.

Inside the house, juniors slept five or six to a room. The roof above the senior boys' dormitories leaked badly when it rained. After I'd joined them, I heard one of the boys joke that we at least had running water in all our rooms. Following a particularly big downpour we sometimes had to move our mattresses into the classroom below. Conditions for the female pupils, who slept in a different building but shared classes with us until the sixth grade, were better.

Our days started at six in the morning. We woke up, washed, made our beds and lined up for breakfast at seven. As we grew older, we had a study hour before breakfast. Getting out of bed was especially difficult during the winter months when it would be still quite dark and we would be snuggling and warm in our beds in the unheated dormitory. Our breakfast generally consisted of labaneh (partly dehydrated yogurt), olive oil and a mixture of herbs and spices called zaatar. At other times, we had bread with three kinds of home-made jam, prune, grape and apricot. The last was my favourite, but other pupils felt differently. Bored with the jam routine, one of my fellow pupils one day wrote a little Arabic ditty to express this: 'Jam, jam, each morning at daybreak, dear Miss Mary this gives me a belly ache.' (Miss Mary, one of the five Nasir sisters teaching at the school, was in charge of food.)

In fact, we had little to complain about. There was fresh hot milk (to which we could add cocoa brought from home) and we were also served eggs twice a week. Lunch usually consisted of rice and a stew made of seasonal vegetables cooked with some meat. The dishes were brought in from the main building by the school's maids, who carried them on their heads for the 300-yard walk to the dining room.

The maids also prepared dough in the kitchen, which was then baked in the traditional village oven. As they walked back, we would sometimes jump up and snatch one of the freshly baked loaves from the baskets on their heads. Although this was forbidden, the maids tolerated our behaviour, at least while we were small, because the hot bread was delicious, much nicer than the bread offered with our meals, which was often stale, so that we didn't eat very much of it.

Birzeit was renowned for its good food, and especially for serving rice, which was not easily available during the Second World War. The school would buy it from farms in the upper Jordan Valley near Bisan. Different parts of Palestine had different soil and lay in different climatic zones; because of this, farmers grew a variety of crops. Palestine was never a desert.

At 3 o'clock every afternoon, we would all go for a country walk to the village of Birzeit. During winter and spring, we would also go flower-picking in the wild meadows. The village was surrounded by low hills flecked in green, brown and red as far as the eye could see. Some of the landscape was unchanged since biblical times. Starting in November, we would collect narcissi, which grew in profusion at the end of the old Jaffa Road by a small copse called Al-Hursh. Until 1948, a bus passed daily from Jaffa on this road going to Jerusalem. It passed through the village of Salameh and Birzeit and many other Arab villages. Salameh was ethnically cleansed in 1948 and on its land the main campus of Tel Aviv University was built.

February and March were the season for wild tulips, best found at the valley near Attara. Red and coloured anemones would appear in Al-Marj, just before you reach Birzeit (where the current university campus has been built) and in the area near Jifna. It was our country and we loved it.

In March there would be an annual competition among different schools organised in cooperation with the Palestine Horticultural Society. Prizes were handed out for the best wild flower

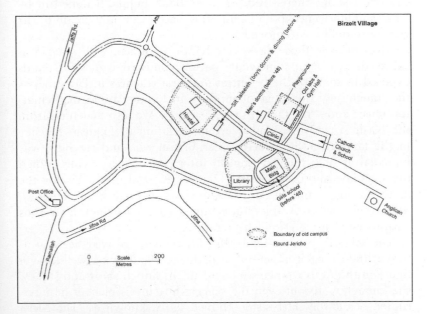

Map 2 Plan of Birzeit Village and old campus, 1930s to 1960s

arrangements, focusing on the variety of plants. Birzeit's pupils almost always won that competition. Our arrangements would include anemones of all colours, orchids of a local variety known as Nahle (bee), wild honeysuckle (which we called 'wild jasmine'), ranunculus and cyclamen, as well as tulips and narcissi.

My favourite walk was the road that went in the direction of the small village of Burham. We liked this road because it was lined with huge flat boulders on which we could run and hop from one boulder to another. I especially liked the presence of a few trees interspersed between these boulders. On Sundays we would often go for picnics. One of the most beautiful picnic sites was Al-Saqi on the Attara Road. Not only did it have an old orchard still producing fruit but a spring on the site fed into several cool ponds. However, the site I liked best was in Jalazon. It had shady trees, climbing rocks and a spring which would spout tiny waterfalls in the early part of the year. (Today, Jalazon is the site of the West Bank's largest refugee camp).

When we got older, we could roam further afield. Birzeit was on the road to Ramallah, then a small hill town whose coolness in the summer months made it a popular location for Arab holiday homes. At weekends, we were sometimes allowed to visit friends or go to the sweet shops there. Today's West Bank pupils, hemmed in by Israel's military checkpoints and army bases, can only dream of the carefree mobility we enjoyed.

Most of us in those days were happy at Birzeit, with our physical needs met, if in somewhat spartan conditions, and our minds exposed to some of the brightest and best teachers in Palestine, as they taught us a full range of subjects, including Arabic, mathematics, music and – my favourite – chemistry. We also benefited from the Nasir sisters' love and deep appreciation of English. Fluency in the language was valued under British rule and teaching was bilingual at first, then in English for all secondary classes. When the mandate authorities in 1942 allowed students to sit for the matriculation exams in Arabic as well as in English and Hebrew, Birzeit switched to Arabic, but retained the higher English syllabus with its emphasis on English literature.

The school's principal, Nabiha Nasir, had received her education at the Evangelical School in Bethlehem and was a well-known figure in the Arab women's movement. Although short and stocky, she knew how to put even the biggest boy in his place if he interrupted her lesson. Her sister Ni'meh Faris, known as 'The Mrs', was a strict but truly brilliant English teacher. I owe my grasp of the language and my deep enjoyment of Shakespeare to her. Yet another sister, Najla Nasir, taught the middle years, while Aniseh taught the kindergarten and the first and second year primary class. And Mary was not just responsible for the food but also introduced us to drama and dance.

Other activities helped pupils to develop their minds. Every Wednesday afternoon, we had what was known as Khitabeh, elocution or oration, a session in which we alternated between English and Arabic oration and recitation. Students would recite poems and sometimes read their own compositions or literary pieces. At the end of the year, there would be a competition in which some of these pieces would be performed. The best poem, piece of prose and recital would receive awards. The adjudicators for the highly popular annual poetry competition usually came from outside the school. Each year, students waited impatiently for this day.

Saturday evenings were for socials involving group games, conversation and listening to music. Sometimes students would perform dramatic scenes or sketches. Occasionally, we would also act out complete Arabic or international plays, including some by Shakespeare. Since these 'social evenings' were not usually mixed, the roles of females had to be played by male students and vice versa in the girls' school. When my voice was still a soprano, I was once cast as a woman in an Arabic play. I went on to play Robin Hood and other parts in performances we gave in Jerusalem and other Palestinian towns.

Ours were modest productions, since the school had no theatre and the stage had to be improvised by pushing together a group of dining tables and covering them with rugs. Still, the preparations alone generated much excitement. What we senior boys liked even more was to visit Birzeit's senior girls' school in order to attend the plays performed by its students.

In addition, a music teacher would come once a week to Birzeit to give piano lessons and coach the school choir. In the 1940s we were lucky to have Salvador Arnita, who was the most outstanding Palestinian musician, the YMCA's organist and the conductor of the Palestine Symphony Orchestra at the YMCA on Sundays. The little school car used to collect Arnita at the Ein Senia junction, since he came in the early morning. Arnita not only coached the choir but also composed special pieces for it, including settings for lyrics from some national poets.

On Sundays, Christian students would be led to the Anglican Church in Birzeit. Church was obligatory, but I used to enjoy it anyway because of the hymns and songs, which were quite different from those of the Greek Orthodox Church. Sometimes Muslim students also came along. After church, male students who had sisters in the school were allowed to go and visit them at the girls' school for an hour – one more, greatly appreciated, a chance to meet the other sex.

There were two other major events reflecting the diversity of Birzeit's student body. One was the field day, held on the main football pitch near Jifna just before the end-of-year exams. This saw contests among four teams, whose names represented the four Islamic leaders of armies which fought during the early Islamic conquests: Muthanna Ibnu Haritha (black flag), Khaled Ibn Al-Waleed (green flag), Saad Ibn Abi Waqqas (red flag) and Usama Ibn Zaid (white flag). The colours are also those of the Palestinian flag. All would compete in 'track and field' events, including jumping, running and gymnastics. The winning team would receive a cup, usually presented by a well-known figure in the community. It was a jolly, festive occasion which the people of Birzeit village would also attend, along with many of the boarders' parents, taking a chance to visit their children.

The annual graduation ceremony was another happy occasion. The choir would sing national and popular songs, and in the 1940s Salvador Arnita would bring members of the Palestine Symphony Orchestra to perform with it. Moreover, the girls would give a highly enjoyable dancing performance, choreographed by Mary Nasir. At the end of the day, public figures from the Palestinian community would hand out the graduation certificates.

All this reflected the school's broader ambition to form the character of its students and advance the development of the Palestinian people. Many of our activities were confidence building, but we were also taught that the public good must come before personal gain. National aspirations and patriotism were encouraged by our teachers. Some were affiliated to the Arab National Movement, which sought to raise the Arab nation as a whole from its state of under-development. Birzeit was a secular, national school and its graduates stood out not just academically but also in terms of their human and leadership values.

By the 1940s, our hopeful vision of a future without foreign rule was heading for a sharp knock. In towns and along major transport routes, tensions between Palestinians and the Zionists who claimed Palestine as their homeland were coming to the boil. There were ambushes, raids and bombings. The Irgun, an illegal Zionist organisation, blew up the King David Hotel in Jerusalem, killing 91 people, including 41 Arabs, 28 British citizens and 17 Jews.

Between 1944 and 1946 there was a water shortage in the school, and the administration decided to take the boarders to Jerusalem on Saturdays, to spend the day at the YMCA to swim and have our hot showers (our weekly bath) there. In my case, I usually took the opportunity to visit my parents along with some of my friends. On rare occasions, we would be taken to a film, including certain classics like *Gone with the Wind* and *A Song to Remember* (on the life of Chopin). Walking around, I also became intrigued by the city's sights: narrow alleys lined with fragrant spice booths would end in lush private gardens; the pale stonework of cupolas and church spires would be turned gold by an August sunset. Otherwise, we were rarely given permission to leave the school premises, even to visit our parents, whom we could only visit during the regular vacations, one in winter and the other in spring and the long summer vacation. We waited for Sundays when our parents would come and bring some presents such as snacks that we were allowed to keep in special boxes in the snack room.

Unfortunately, in our class of 1946 there were only seven boys and around seven girls. We could not have a graduation ceremony that year but it was combined in the following year with the class of 1947 at a big ceremony at the YMCA hall in Jerusalem rather than in Birzeit.

But events were to take a serious turn. As tensions between Palestinians and Zionist forces rose, the British withdrew. Taking over the mandate, the United Nations, in which the Palestinians were not represented, voted to create two states out of mandate Palestine, one for the Jews and one for the Palestinian Arabs. It was presented to the world as 'sharing' a state to which both groups had equal claim, even though the country had always had a large majority of Arabs – over 90 per cent at the time of the Balfour Declaration. So the world body imposed a division of their country on the Palestinian people, who were never consulted about it. When it was clear that the Zionists were not even respecting the generous borders that had been allocated to them, armies from neighbouring Arab countries moved in to protect the Palestinians and preserve the territorial integrity of Palestine. The war of 1948 resulted in the loss of 78 per cent of historic Palestine to the new Jewish state, the remaining 22 per cent being the West Bank (including East Jerusalem) and the Gaza Strip.

According to the UN plan, my home city, Jerusalem, was meant

to be shared by both sides under UN trusteeship, but as a result of
the war our house, in west Jerusalem, was on the Israeli side and
thus unreachable.

My father was to pine all his life for this home he had created
with so much care. Looking down on it from the East Jerusalem
YMCA rooftop with me, he assured me that we would get it back
some day. What we got, eventually, was a chance to stand outside
its front door. After the Six-Day War in 1967, Israel occupied all of
Jerusalem, and my father was able to visit his house at last. When
he arrived there, he found that the house had been badly damaged
by shelling in 1948. Worse, it now had an Israeli army reservist
as a squatter and was under the auspices of the Israeli 'Custodian
of Absentee Property'. When my father presented himself at this
government department, he was told that he could not reclaim the
property as he was an 'absentee'. My father, a tall, well-built man,
failed to see how anyone could consider him 'absent', given his
indisputable presence.

He went on to file a claim for the house, but was informed that
we would only get it back when there was peace between Palestinians and Israelis. When he asked if he could at least rent it, he was
fobbed off with ever-changing excuses. One official claimed that
it was unfit for habitation. My father replied that, as an architect,
he was undoubtedly able to restore it. Nevertheless, he was not
allowed to set foot in the house again to his dying day.

In 1948, though, none of us could have imagined such an
outcome. The UN had allocated 55 per cent of Palestine to a
Jewish state, although Jews owned about 6 per cent of the area of
Palestine and made up only a third of its population in 1947, even
after massive illegal immigration from Europe. In spite of the moral
support of the rest of the Arab world, the poorly equipped Arab
forces suffered crushing defeats. Israeli army units advanced almost
unopposed into the heart of the country until they had occupied
78 per cent of it. Palestinians themselves had no army nor, in most
cases, weapons of any sort to stop them. A wave of ethnic cleansing
swept through central Palestine. Decades later, Israeli Prime Minister Yitzhak Rabin would admit in his autobiography that when his
forces had entered Ramleh in 1948, they had given the Palestinian
town's inhabitants a stark choice: they could get on the trucks waiting outside their homes and be driven to a place still controlled by
their own side – or to risk being forcibly removed and then walk.

After the massacre of 254 men women and children in the
village of Deir Yassin outside Jerusalem, carried out by the forces

of another future Israeli prime minister, Menahem Begin, no Palestinian felt safe. People from Jaffa and the neighbouring southern villages escaped south to Gaza, while to the east the people of Ramleh and Lydda and the northern villages walked eastward through the mountains and took refuge in Ramallah and Birzeit, unless they were able to leave for Lebanon by boat.

As a result, the Birzeit area was flooded with tens of thousands of refugees. Obliged to carry children or help old people, many arrivals brought with them only the clothes they stood in. Conditions were atrocious. Almost every olive tree had a homeless family living under it. The idyllic world we had grown up in had suddenly disappeared.

2

PEACE AND WAR

My own life appeared to be set on a smoother course. I had graduated with distinction some time before what we came to call the Nakba, the Arabic word for catastrophe, and I had been encouraged by my family to continue with higher education. My father was eager for me to embark on a career in medicine, but I was determined to study chemistry. Chemical reactions fascinated me and I saw myself becoming an industrial chemist in a science laboratory, developing valuable new products. Palestine was rich in fruit and vegetables, for example, but we needed to find ways to process them. The future, all young people felt, lay in industrialisation.

It was a decision which led to lots of domestic arguments, but I was lucky to be supported by a family friend who had studied chemistry. He eventually managed to persuade my father that I should be allowed to choose my own field (an idea not yet current among Arab parents). 'It does not matter what you study,' he said, 'as long as you enjoy your subject because, this way, you are bound to excel.' Years later, I found myself quoting these lines whenever parents anxiously begged me for advice about their children's choice of university course.

Palestine had no Arab university and so my father and I, having settled on a chemistry course, travelled to Beirut. My first experience of it was eye-opening. Beirut was a modern Mediterranean city, a meeting point of East and West. It was multicultural and multiconfessional and lacked the austere atmosphere of Jerusalem. There were restaurants, cabarets, bars and other establishments catering for a public that enjoyed life and seemingly didn't care about money. Downtown Beirut was a place in which people spoke French as much as Arabic, while English dominated in the neighbourhood of the American University of Beirut, my new alma mater, known as AUB.

I threw myself into university life with gusto. The AUB offered stimulating lectures and exciting practicals. In the holidays, I went skiing for the first time ever in the Cedar Mountains. Later, some Lebanese fellow students took me on a camping trip into the Druze mountains, as one of them had family there. I was fascinated by the area's lush greenery, profusion of springs and pure air, all of which had gained Lebanon the nickname 'little Switzerland'.

Life, though, was about to change. My parents, who had been staying with relatives in Birzeit during the 1948 hostilities, found that they had lost not just their home but every asset acquired during my father's working life. They could no longer support me. Nor could they pay for me to return home.

Having just gained my chemistry BA, I had hoped to continue my studies. This now looked impossible, as I was penniless. What I needed urgently was to start earning, but jobs of any sort were hard to find in Lebanon, especially if you were a foreigner. From a relatively privileged student, I had become an exile, part of the huge mass of uprooted Palestinians in that small country.

By the end of that summer, the AUB's Dean of the School of Arts and Sciences, who happened to be a member of my department, offered me a job as a chemistry instructor. This provided me with a stable if modest income. When the AUB's Master's programme was launched I eagerly joined it, completing the course in 1953.

AUB had not just given me a worthwhile qualification but a chance to meet new people, among them Lebanese, Iraqis, Syrians, Palestinians and Americans. The question of what to do next resolved itself as soon as I saw an advertisement on the AUB notice-board which invited staff members to apply for jobs in Birzeit's Junior College programme. In 1953, I was accepted and returned, delighted to be in its familiar environment again. A great deal had changed, though.

For a start, Birzeit, and the whole of the West Bank, were yet again under different rule. Having been under the British administration, we were now subjects of the Hashemite Kingdom of Jordan, which had assumed responsibility for the part of Palestine that covered the West Bank of the Jordan but had not really made its affairs a priority.

In this situation, the school had struggled even to keep going after 1948. There were far fewer boarders and total student numbers had dwindled. Generally, the region's economic situation was poor. The influx of refugees had also brought changes, though the worst of the crisis was over. Musa Nasir had worked with the Red Cross to help them survive during those difficult early years. Eventually the refugees were placed into camps both in Birzeit and neighbouring areas like Deir Ammar and Jalazon, chosen because there was fresh water there. Two other refugee camps sprang up in nearby Ramallah/El Bireh (Qaddoura and El Am'ari). UNWRA started to provide elementary schooling for the refugees' children.

After a while, families who could afford it began to rent accommodation in Ramallah. This was not always easy to find and the town began to expand as new houses (each no taller than four floors according to local rules) were built for the newcomers. Ramallah was slowly expanding towards the northern edge of Jerusalem, the cultural and business centre of its inhabitants. There was another significant change: while Ramallah had originally been a Christian town, it was now mixed Christian and Muslim. Still, it maintained a secular, open society, partly because in this way it could draw in more tourists.

These gradual changes prevented Birzeit from going under. With the death of Nabiha Nasir, her brother, Musa Nasir, formally took over the reins and began to look for ways in which more students might be attracted and stay on longer. His first step had been to enable them to sit for the advanced level of the General Certificate of Education (GCE) in certain subjects. His second step was to seek help from abroad.

In 1952 a delegation from the Ford Foundation, which was looking for educational projects to benefit the Palestinian people, visited Birzeit. Discussions between them and its staff led to the idea of starting a junior college which would offer students a two-year higher education programme. Successful participants would be able to continue their education at the AUB or a similar institution and so gain a BA. Teaching would have to be done in English, because all learning materials were in that language, but students unable to pass the English exam would not be discriminated against. Instead, they would be put into an intensive English programme and coached in arts and sciences terminology. Musa Nasir submitted the proposal, the Ford Foundation accepted it and Birzeit received its first grant.

It was this project which had created the need for new, academically qualified staff, and when I arrived I drew on my AUB experience to introduce new methods of teaching and administration. From now on, science students would be encouraged to experiment, not just cram scientific facts. To make this possible, with the help of the Ford Foundation the school invested in proper laboratories for chemistry, biology and physics. A library for reference books and journals was also created.

The author (right) during coffee break at the staff room with Musa Nasir and Munir Nasser, 1962

One of my students in those years, now a renowned international scientist, likes to remind me how I showed his class that solar energy could be harnessed when I demonstrated to them that an egg could be boiled in water from the sun's rays, reflected and focused by a parabolic mirror, and then played them a radio powered by solar cells. This inspired him and gave him the idea of a solar-powered airship. He developed the idea, calculated a proof of concept, and then presented his findings in the British journal *New Scientist* and at a conference at the Royal Aeronautical Society in London. Solar-powered airships are now considered seriously for telecommunication and surveillance operations in the stratosphere, 20 kilometres above sea level, where only solar energy is available.

I had not started off with a vocation for teaching, but found that I could inspire young people and gained a huge amount of pleasure from this. Samia Nasir, who had just come back from the United States after getting her BA in business administration from Southwestern University, helped to reorganise the school's administration, admissions process and management. Her changes would allow the college to be efficient, fair and capable of implementing new ideas

Musa Nasir's son, Hanna, who had also studied abroad, was equally keen to innovate. Together, we started Birzeit's science

Science Fair with solar heater and telescope, 1963

fair. Each year, it was attended by busloads of high-school pupils from both sides of the River Jordan, as well as by local villagers. In order to create an interesting display, we'd work all night in our lab along with our college students. We mainly offered demonstrations or experiments that the pupils had no chance of seeing at their own schools, but we would add a few visual science tricks for excitement.

Not only did this project increase the interest in science among the pupils, but the achievements of our college students rose as their involvement increased.

New students had some adjustments to make. Many traditional schools relied on rote learning, but we were keen to teach our students to think beyond the normal limits in their subjects. On walks and camping trips, Birzeit staff would discuss ethical issues with the students in both English and Arabic, and encourage them to develop flexible minds and to speak up. They could voice their views directly to the administration or via the college billboards and *Al-Ghadeer*, the student paper. Democratic voting practices were fostered by holding Student Council elections.

The next step was to improve the students' environment. Now that Birzeit was admitting older, more sophisticated candidates, it needed better-quality housing and proper sporting facilities. Birzeit's pupils had played football or netball on grass, but the Ford Foundation grant paid for volleyball and basketball courts. However, our attempts to buy plots for academic buildings met with suspicion from Palestinian villagers. They were reluctant to sell their land because they had heard about the grant and accused us of planning to build a Ford car factory.

We also purchased some seedlings and held a tree planting ceremony. Seeing college students and lecturers hold a spade and dig holes in the ground shocked some parents, but it was a lesson in the value of physical work. It eventually created a shaded and much appreciated pine grove for our campus. The trees' sole enemies were the grazing animals nearby, which would eat the new leaves. Visitors were often greeted by the sight of a dignified, be-suited staff member breathlessly chasing a group of goats with a blackboard pointer.

A bigger headache was accreditation, which had to come from a recognised university. The AUB, then the main establishment attended by Palestinian and Jordanian students, was not eager to grant it. Their staff preferred students to come directly to Lebanon rather than spend the first two years of their degree course elsewhere. Parents, on the other hand, liked their children to study at Birzeit first, as it was cheaper and they knew that the quality of education was just as good. But proving our merit took several years. The AUB only relented after comparing the grades obtained by our transfer students in its third year with those of its own cohort and finding that our students as a group did much better. By 1962, we had become an accredited academic institution.

Our relationship with the Jordanian Ministry of Education could also be challenging. Its officials maintained a rather negative attitude towards Birzeit, as they did not like educational bodies independent of their government. They were also aware that we saw ourselves as a Palestinian national institution in terms of identity and allegiances.

What eventually improved relations with the Jordanians was a new project. In 1960, we obtained funds from the US Agency for International Development (USAID) for a two-year programme leading to the associate degree in public administration. Musa Nasir had always maintained that, just like other professions, civil servants needed to be trained and specialised, and he wanted to help the Jordanian government with this. We took on 30 students on full scholarship and were able to recruit highly qualified teaching staff from the United States. The students were selected by the government, but we ensured that they met our basic entrance requirements. The programme was a success and many of its graduates were immediately employed either by the Jordanian government or in banking.

Pleased with Birzeit's achievements in the higher education field, we decided to phase out the high-school programme. It had been very popular, but we wanted to focus on developing minds beyond this stage, especially within our community.

My personal life was looking up too. In 1964 I married Haifa, a young teacher from Gaza, who had been working in a refugee school there. Her support and understanding soon proved invaluable to me, though she would scold me for working excessively long hours. When riled, she would half-jokingly say that Birzeit was really my first (senior) wife, while she was my second. Still, we were extremely happy; our first child, Hania, was born in February 1966 and in the spring of 1967 Haifa was expecting our second child. Things could only get better, we thought.

But we were wrong. The Six Day War broke out in the midst of the finals exams. On Monday, 5 June 1967 at 8.30 am the students were just entering the examination rooms when my friend Wadi' Nasir ran up to me. Wadi', the brother of the famous Palestinian poet Kamal Nasir who was later assassinated by the Israelis in Beirut, had alarming news: 'Eighty Israeli planes have been downed! The Israelis claim they have shot down lots of Egyptian planes and they are entering the Sinai. Fighting has started!'

We had been afraid that there was going to be war, as tensions had been steadily rising. Six months earlier, the Israeli Army had occupied the village of Samou' near Hebron, blown up a dozen houses and killed several people before withdrawing again. There were border incidents and violent clashes. Demonstrators in Jordan demanded action and two days earlier, the Jordanian army had held a parade in Ramallah. It had included a tank and a field gun but the local people had not been impressed, suspecting that these two weapons might be all that was available. Then President Nasser of Egypt asked the UN troops stationed as a buffer zone in the Sinai to leave, and the UN complied. The Straits of Tiran in the Gulf of Aqaba were closed to Israeli shipping. Israel let it be known that it regarded this as a threat to its existence. A major confrontation seemed inevitable.

Still, West Bankers were not taking the situation too seriously. We were civilians and did not have a military mentality. With Jordan in control of our territory, Palestinians acted only as border guards. They would be given five bullets each and an antiquated gun which they were not allowed to use. People told themselves that the worst that might happen would be for the Israelis to storm two or three places, fire a few rounds as they'd done before, then leave again.

So normality was the order of the day. My brother George had arranged to be married on 4 June in the Greek Orthodox Church on the Mount of Olives, then a strategic location from which the Jordanian military could overlook Jerusalem. His friends advised him to cancel the wedding as the hill would by then be awash with Jordanian soldiers but he refused. This proved to be a wise decision because on 3 June the entire Jordanian unit left. When I arrived at the church the next day with Haifa, who was nine months pregnant, there was ample parking space.

Now, though, war had started for real and we later discovered that the newlyweds never got a honeymoon. As their plane was about to take off for Italy, the Israelis bombed the airport, passengers had to disembark and the couple struggled to get back from Jordan. They took a taxi to Bethany, breaking for lunch with a priest they knew, then walked from there to their house by the Palestine Museum (now the Rockefeller Museum) in Jerusalem. There they would crawl under their bed whenever they heard Israeli soldiers pass, which was rather often. It became a family joke that they spent their honeymoon under the bed, not on it.

Their disappointing experience in the end turned out to be a stroke of luck. What we didn't know then was that if they had stayed away any longer, they would have been permanently banned from re-entering by Israel. Stranded abroad like many Palestinians in 1967, they too would have become 'absentees'.

All this, though, was still in the future. 'Please do not shout,' I told Wadi'. 'Our students need to complete their exams; we can't make a fuss.' Soon we started getting telephone calls from Amman. Almost half our boarders came from the Jordanian capital on the East Bank and worried parents were asking 'What will happen to our children?' I tried to calm them. Tomorrow was the last day of exams and it was important that students stayed to the end. 'After that,' I said, 'come and collect them.'

By 10.30 am, though, families started to arrive from Amman, determined to take their children home. By 11 am the students had finished at least the first exam session and, at the insistence of the parents, we let them go. Fortunately, all the boarders made it home, because the bridges across the Jordan River remained open until midday.

Meanwhile, there was a problem over what to do with the students from Jerusalem. News started coming that it was becoming difficult to reach the city by car and so we decided to put them on a bus. Half an hour later, they were back in Birzeit. The bus had been turned back near Jerusalem, at Shu'fat, by Jordanian soldiers who said it was too dangerous to drive on. So the students would have to stay in Birzeit. There were over 40 of them and we put them up in the college dormitories. As a boarding school, we had enough food supplies for a few days, but the day students were shaken by the events, and also had nothing with them except their clothes.

I then took home in the college van the small group of students living in the neighbouring Ramallah villages. Just before we reached Beit Hanina we saw a crushed car by the side of the road, which had apparently been rammed by a heavy vehicle. Later, when such damage became a common sight, we learned to identify its cause as an Israeli tank or armoured car.

Having dealt with these problems, I could now focus on my own family. My sister Laura was on her own with four children since her husband, a doctor working in Bethlehem, was unable to get home, so I took them to stay with us.

Laura was welcomed by Haifa, who was expected to give birth that week. Haifa's brother, Dr Antone Tarazi, was stationed in the

Science Fair: high school students watching a physics experiment, 1963

Jordanian Military Hospital at Beitin and had arranged a bed for her there. The next day, though, he had to tell her that the arrangement had fallen through. The hospital was closed as all the Jordanian army personnel had been withdrawn.

Dr Tarazi had arranged for Haifa to give birth in the Ramallah hospital instead, but the town was becoming unsafe. Ramallah had a popular radio station, and in the afternoon there was an Israeli air raid on its antennas. We were terrified because the plane came and shot up the whole area. Dr Tarazi's own home was hit, as was the home of Vera Tamari, one of our lecturers. Two little girls standing outside the town's YMCA were killed and their teacher injured. You can still see the shell marks on the building today.

Complications in Haifa's pregnancy added another worry. Her gynaecologist, Dr Issam Nazer, predicted that she might need a Caesarean, for which the hospital in Ramallah was poorly equipped. He therefore felt she ought to be delivered at his own maternity hospital in Nabi Ya'coub (Neveh Yacov) near Jerusalem.

I remember the following day, Wednesday, 7 June 1967, very well because it was Haifa's birthday. We were sleeping on mattresses on our basement floor, as we had no other shelter. When we woke up early in the morning, I smiled and wished her a 'Happy Birthday!' It was a strange situation, as we had barely slept and it certainly was not a happy occasion. Around 5 am, our neighbour, who had been staying with us in the shelter, rushed in and announced: 'Yakhti Im Gabi dakhalul yahud' ('dear Im Gabi the Jews have entered'). It was shocking news. We had lost the rest of Palestine.

None of the Jordanian or Egyptian news channels we had listened to had prepared us for this outcome. We'd only guessed the bad news when King Hussein of Jordan himself came on air and declared: 'Attack them with whatever you have, and if you do not have knives or weapons, attack them with your nails and teeth.' As the first army vehicles arrived in Ramallah later that day, some local people still thought this was the Iraqi Army, coming to aid the Jordanians. Some people run up to welcome them and got shot. They realised too late that these were Israelis.

The Israelis call this 'The Six Day War', but there was no war. 'Six-day Promenade' is more like it. In most parts of the West Bank except Jenin, there was no fighting, no resistance, nothing. Israeli soldiers were walking into this house and that house, taking what they wanted. Men who had worn the Jordanian army uniform took it off and disappeared among the people.

My parents, my sister and her children, as well as Haifa carrying the unborn child, our son Hani, were all cooped up in the house with me. We watched through the window as a group of soldiers in jeeps tried to start a Volkswagen belonging to one of our neighbours. Then a few of the soldiers turned and walked up to our house. They were carrying guns.

'Are these really Jews, and are they really Israelis?' I thought. Not only had we never seen an Israeli Jew in Ramallah, but our information about Jews in general was minimal. Books about Israel had been banned and although some must have been available clandestinely, they were very hard to get hold of. What were we to expect?

When I opened the door, one of the soldiers pointed his gun at me. I am sure I looked deadly pale. Old stories flashed into my mind: Haifa had told me about what had happened in 1956, when the Israeli army entered Gaza. In many cases, the Israelis had lined up the men of the house and shot them in front of their families. So by the time I reached the door, the blood had drained from my face.

The soldier addressed me in Arabic 'La tkhaf (Do not be afraid), we're not going to shoot.' 'What is it that you want?' I asked. 'Is there anyone else in the house with you?' he said. 'Yes,' I said. 'My wife, my parents, my sister and her four little children.' He ordered them all out, onto the veranda, and the soldiers went into the house. They searched it for a while, then came out again.

The soldiers had been quite polite and so my mother said to them 'Can I make you some tea?' They replied: 'No, we've got beer.' When they had gone we went inside and discovered that they had helped themselves to the beer from our fridge. Unfortunately, we later found out that they had also taken all my mother's jewellery, a golden pen that belonged to Haifa, a pair of binoculars and some gold coins my father had kept. Usually he kept the coins and jewellery under lock and key, but that day he hadn't. The pockets of the soldiers' trousers had been big enough to hide anything. Haifa had kept all her jewellery and our money on her belt. She had learnt to do this after the Israelis had entered the Gaza Strip in 1956 and had told my sister to do the same. My mother, alas, had thought that my father's little box was safe.

Having one's home looted, which was to become a standard feature of the occupation, was only one of several unpleasant new experiences. In the afternoon, another soldier walked into our house and demanded the keys of our car. It was a one-month-old Peugeot 404, our first car, and we had only paid the first instalment. Parked alongside it was my brother's car, a Volkswagen Beetle, which he'd left with us before going on his honeymoon. As it was quite old, the

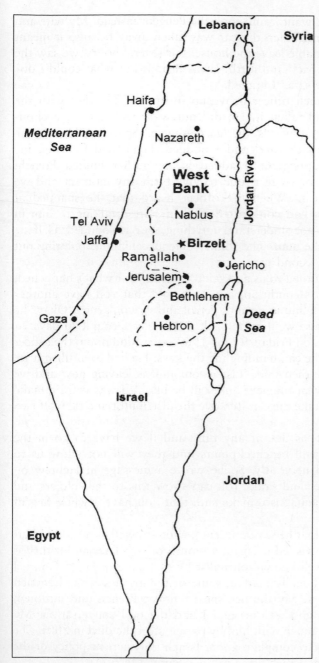

Map 3 Birzeit in the West Bank

soldiers did not want it and took the Peugeot instead. My wife and sister were crying when the car was taken away because it meant we would be unable leave the house. For several hours, we saw the soldier drive it back and forth. I was furious but what could I do? 'At least we are safe,' I argued.

Later, an Israeli officer drove up in our car together with the soldier who had taken it. He did not want to come in, beckoning me instead towards the garden gate. Speaking French, he asked: 'Is this your car?' and I nodded. Haifa had followed me out, obviously pregnant. I added in my rather limited French: 'Unfortunately, my wife is due to give birth any moment and we will need the car.' When the officer heard that, he snapped at the soldier who had confiscated it, then started talking to him in Hebrew. I did not understand anything, but it sounded as if he was rebuking the man. The soldier defended himself, pointing out that we had a second car.

The officer turned to us and said, 'I'm sorry for what's happened, given your wife's condition, but I am told that you have another car.' 'Yes,' I said, 'but it is out of petrol and so won't run.' 'Okay,' he replied, 'I promise we'll bring back this one in a couple of days.'

Sure enough, on Friday, 9 June 1967, at around noon, the officer returned with the car, handing me the keys. He had even filled it up with petrol. He then said, 'Listen, our unit is leaving now and we do not know what the next unit will be like. If I was you I'd make sure they can't take the car. Remove the distributor and take off two of the wheels.'

'But my wife is due at any time and if we have to go in the evening, there will be checkpoints and they will not allow us to pass!' I replied nervously. So he wrote a message in Hebrew on a piece of paper and said, 'You can show this to the soldiers and they will help you. Also, make sure that you have a white flag of some kind.'

We realised that he was a decent person, as well as a rather interesting man. He visited us again a month or two later and it turned out he was a well-known journalist by the name of Haim Gouri. I ended up occasionally reading some of the articles he had written in Israeli papers. My mother speaks fluent French and although mine is not as good, Gouri and I had the odd conversation. My mother kept in touch with him by phone until she died in 2001. She would call him to complain about Israeli government policy or the behaviour of the Israeli army in the occupied territories.

That afternoon, we heeded his advice and took the wheels off

Gabi and Haifa Baramki, 2006

the car. At midnight however, Haifa decided that the baby was due. As the electricity was cut off, I had to go down to the garage with a candle to put the wheels back on again. I then started to drive although I could hardly see. There was a blackout, all the houses were dark and our headlights were painted blue. We improvised a white flag out of a handkerchief and a stick so that the soldiers wouldn't shoot at us despite the curfew. Haifa held the flag and waved it out of the window. We were both in tears, aware that getting to the hospital might be a matter of life or death.

On the way to Ramallah, we were stopped at the checkpoint outside the old Radio Station now occupied by the Israelis. We showed them the paper I got from Gouri and, sure enough, the soldier who read it became helpful. 'Wait here,' he said. 'You can't go to the centre of town because there is a tank blocking it. If you try to pass, they will shoot first and ask questions later.' So a jeep drove ahead of us through Ramallah. As we approached Al-Manara Square, which was a small, grass-covered roundabout, we saw that there was indeed a tank in the middle of it. The jeep took us right up to Jerusalem.

When we arrived at Dr Nazer's hospital, the soldier tried to make himself useful by banging on the door with the rifle butt. Nobody answered. The doctor's home was opposite, so we went over and shouted, 'Dr Nazer, Dr Nazer!' but the windows were dark and there was no answer. 'Shall I take you to the Hadassah hospital in West Jerusalem?' asked the soldier. I thanked him but declined. 'We've arranged that if this one is not open, Haifa should come back to the Ramallah Hospital'.

So, the soldier drove us back to Ramallah and started banging on the door of the hospital there. I started shouting too and after a while the door opened. The staff said that they had been too scared of the soldiers to open up, until they'd heard my voice. It later transpired that this was exactly what happened at the other hospital.

During the morning of Saturday, 10 June, Dr Issa Salti, the doctor in charge, watched to see if Haifa could deliver normally. By the afternoon he decided to give up, as she wasn't dilating enough. This was especially worrying since the Ramallah Hospital had no actual maternity ward; it did not even have cribs for babies. Fortunately, though, it had an electric generator which had been left by the Jordanian army. Also, Dr Salti was a good surgeon. He performed a Caesarean and our son Hani was born at 5 pm that day.

Rejoicing in the new arrival, we told ourselves that these were unusual times. Soon, at least a degree of normality would be restored. No other young family would have to go through the terrifying experiences we'd had.

What we could not have imagined was that 40 years later Palestinian women in labour would still be confined to their homes by curfews or running the gauntlet of checkpoints, soldiers and tanks. The human cost of such policies has been terrible. Between 2000 and 2006 alone 39 Palestinian babies and five mothers died because they could not reach medical care in time. As cars are held up for hours at checkpoints or turned back, women are forced to give birth on the back seat or in fields, sometimes within sight of the hospital that could offer them care.

Haifa herself went through the experience of giving birth under occupation once again, each time knowing that unless she was given a Caesarean she might die. Once pregnant, she would shake with fear each time a jeep passed our house. Today, she is involved in a scheme which aims to equip midwives for our extreme circumstances. They are being encouraged to handle even complex and dangerous births in people's homes. Palestinians, apparently, have no right to use hospitals.

3

OCCUPATION AND EDUCATION

Living under Israeli rule was unlike anything we had ever known. For a start, we were now under a military government. The local military governor, an Israeli brigadier, was our chief, but any soldier carrying a gun was a Palestinian's superior. Military orders poured forth, setting out what we could and could not do. To repair your house, raise chickens or plant a tree now required an Israeli permit.

At the same time, Palestinians could be moved around at will in the pursuit of some obscure aim. Within months of the 1967 war, thousands of Palestinian farmers living in the Jordan Valley had been expelled across the River Jordan. Religious Jews in skullcaps and prayer shawls started to appear in the countryside, leafing through their bibles to identify spots for what soon became religious settlements (colonies). In the Latrun area, 17 kilometres west of Jerusalem, three villages called Emwas (the biblical Emmaus), Yalo and Beit Nuba were razed to the ground, then replaced by an Israeli leisure facility called Canada Park.

Palestinian were becoming irrelevant in this emerging landscape, almost invisible. As they lost their land, many were reduced to the status of impoverished day labourers, yet even this lowly status seemed to irritate Israelis. One of our students heard a woman touring in a military jeep say to her driver: 'This would be a beautiful land without Arabs.'

Running a college in this atmosphere became a test of patience and determination. When the military governor declared that he would like to inspect our classes, we explained that this was absolutely unacceptable. 'I do not even do so myself,' I told him. Sometimes the officer announced that he wished to see us to discuss certain issues. We would reply: 'We're not happy about this, but will attend the meeting.' It was a military order. However, if the military came to us, we told them not to roam around campus. They had to come straight to the office of the college president.

Gradually, the military took to dropping in whenever they felt like it, but we insisted they give us advance notice. They clearly did not like this, but we felt it was important to draw up some rules to make them respect us. So, an officer would phone first, but then they would drive up and surround the campus with jeeps and soldiers.

This provoked the students, who took to demonstrating with anti-occupation placards. Most of these simply carried the reference numbers of the UN Resolutions Israel had ignored: Resolution 194 of 1948, which stipulated that the refugees wishing to return to their homes should be allowed to do so, and Resolution 242 of 1967, which called for the withdrawal of Israeli forces from territories they had occupied. Although the students were protesting on college sites or marching on the road encircling the town which we called in the olden days 'round Jericho', the military treated such demonstrations as security incidents. They would chase the students and arrest some of them. Then, they would tie the students' hands behind their back with plastic handcuffs that cut deep into the skin, before making them sit on the ground. Anyone who moved or looked up could expect a series of bone-shattering blows with their rifle butts. If any students tried to run off they would be shot at. Still, there was the small mercy that the soldiers did not shoot at the upper parts of students' bodies. This, they knew, might kill.

Peasants resisting Israeli land confiscations, urban youths protesting against the demolition of homes, and refugees returning illegally to their West Bank homes were not accorded such consideration. In the years after 1967, many of them were shot dead.

The Israeli hostility to us escalated when we announced in the summer of 1972 that we would go ahead and develop the two-year programme into a four-year, full degree programme for arts and sciences. Part of the reason for this was practical. Now that West Bankers could no longer easily go to Jordan or Lebanon, we needed a local university. Birzeit was becoming increasingly popular. Students started to come from Gaza, a development we encouraged as we wanted to become a truly national university. We were even admitting students and employing teachers from among the Palestinian minority inside Israel.

Our motives, of course, went beyond compensating for Palestinians' lack of access to universities in the Arab world. We were building a better future for our people. It was not an original idea. Writing in 1852, John Henry (later Cardinal) Newman had spelled out the importance of higher education for another then deeply disadvantaged group, British Catholics. To gain equality, he argued, they needed access to 'the culture of the intellect' which only a proper university could provide. As he wrote then:

> Robbed, oppressed, and thrust aside, Catholics in these islands have not been in a condition for centuries to attempt the sort of education which is necessary for the man of the world, the statesman, the landholder, or the opulent gentleman. Their legitimate stations, duties, employments, have been taken from them, and the qualifications withal, social and intellectual, which are necessary both for reversing the forfeiture and for availing themselves of the reversal. The time is come when this moral disability must be removed.

Despite obvious differences, Newman's argument resonated with us. We needed a university to develop Palestine, train professionals, act as a laboratory for ideas and create a leadership. Education would also enable Palestinians to talk to Israelis on equal terms. As long as our people were not educated, the only possible discourse, we feared, would be by acts of violence.

We also needed to take a long-term view. In 1967, I had still thought that, given international pressure, it would take the Israelis perhaps as much as two years to leave. How wrong I was.

For the 19 years between 1948 and 1967, we Palestinians had said: 'They have taken our land and we are not going to accept that.' Indeed we could not, but it was time to consider the fact that the Israelis were here to stay. I felt that we needed to be able to come to an arrangement with them, whereby we could live in part of Palestine and they could live in another. We could accept the amount of land allocated to us by the United Nations partition plan or instead lay claim to more, though, of course, not settle for less than the 4 June 1967 borders. However, we had to come to terms with the idea that there would be an Israel and a Palestine.

So, if we were destined to be living next to one another, it was better to live in peace than in war. However, you cannot expect an oppressor and the oppressed to coexist. Coexistence required people who were articulate on a large number of subjects, including their rights. By creating a university, we were ensuring that our people would become citizens of an equal stature to the Israelis, so we could live side by side on an equal basis. Birzeit would educate Palestinians to a level at which this could happen.

At the heart of our project was our refusal to accept that we would be 'hewers of wood and carriers of water'. From the start, Israelis had been trying to colonise Palestine so they would have cheap labour for their economy until conditions, both internal and external, would enable them to get rid of the majority of Palestinians. This would enable them to establish a state as Jewish 'as France is French and Britain is British' in the words of its first President, Chaim Weitzman.

In the territories occupied by Israel in 1967, this process was occurring at an accelerated pace. The endless land confiscations were turning rural Palestinians into Israeli day-labourers. These people were the majority of our population and historically most had been farmers, living modestly but independently off their own land. Many had relatively low living standards, but they could not be fully controlled by any government, Israeli or another. It's true that our farmers had often struggled to make ends meet, and they could earn a little more as labourers, but there was a hidden cost. They became dependent on Israel. A labourer is an employee and all you have to do in order to control him is to stop him, or threaten to stop him, from earning. He will be begging for work.

My feeling to this day is that this outcome was deliberate and provided dual benefits for the Israelis. They gained a pool of cheap labour and the money earned by Palestinian labourers was channelled back into the Israeli economy as they bought Israeli goods. However, their jobs could be withdrawn without warning. If meanwhile the labourer had neglected his land, it could have become barren. Left without any source of income, the dispossessed, unemployed farmer had to seek work outside his country. This way, we quickly realised, many of our people were being encouraged to emigrate. Once they had left, moreover, most were not allowed to return.

The more we learnt about the Israelis, the more urgent our university project seemed. Israeli rule was different from anything we had known. The Israelis were seeking to replace us altogether, in subtle and brutal ways. And they were certainly not trying to learn about us, except in the context of 'intelligence gathering'. Hanna and I spent long hours discussing and planning how to go about the Birzeit project. When Hanna became president in 1971, after his father Musa Nasir passed away, we continued with our complementary roles in this enormous endeavour throughout the period following Hanna's deportation until his return and my retirement.

In these threatening circumstances we, the Palestinians, needed to get on with nation-building ourselves. Creating a university was part of this process. It was a road to freedom. Having a university was crucial if we were to resist the occupation. We would produce well-educated, confident graduates, proud of their Palestinian national identity and eager to contribute to the development of their homeland. Moreover, university life would create a haven for the practice of democracy in a situation of political oppression.

This was an idea which resonated with young Palestinian academics dispersed all over the world. Hanan Ashrawi, later one of our most prominent political figures, was completing her PhD at the University of Virginia when she heard of our plans. She immediately applied for a lecturer's job.

Getting accepted by Birzeit quickly proved to be the least of the idealistic young academic's problems. Because Ashrawi had been studying abroad for over a year, the Israelis would not let her live in the West Bank. Although born in Nablus, she was now defined as an 'absentee' and could only come home on a short-term visitor's visa. It would take her father years of persistence in the face of a hostile Israeli bureaucracy to obtain one of a handful of 'family reunion permits' issued by the military for her.

Ashrawi and other new lecturers educated at prestigious foreign universities brought with them new ideas and up-to-date academic practices. They also shared Birzeit's great ambitions for our young people. In 2008, Ashrawi told a British reporter that, at the time, she believed 'this was the only way we could resist the power of Israel's repressive institutions and organisational structures, and instead create our own, more appropriate ones.' She added, 'I was totally committed to academic excellence and thought Palestinians needed academic institutions that were thriving, vigorous and of high standards. A Palestinian university needed to provide a reputable quality of education and I was determined to be one of the people offering that.'

In this spirit, we announced our first full degree courses in the papers, giving dates for the beginning of the academic year and registration. Soon after, we were paid a visit by Israeli Colonel David Farhi, the liaison officer in the office of the Israeli military commander of the West Bank. 'What do you think you are doing?' he asked Hanna and me. We replied matter-of-factly that we were developing our existing courses into a four-year degree programme.

'You can't do that,' he replied. 'You need to first apply for permission.' We answered: 'We are already a college and we do not need a permit.' Farhi insisted that we did.

We tried to stall him, continuing with our arrangements. Four

weeks after his visit, we got a call. We had sent the colonel a letter
that basically informed him of our intentions, rather than applying
for a permit, and he now rejected it. 'That's not what we want. You
must apply, you must get our permission and first we need some
more information,' he told us.

It was the first such case the Israelis ever had to deal with. As
we saw it, there was nothing in the law that said that they were in
charge of higher education. Jordanian law current in 1967, which
applied to us, said that the presiding government is in charge of
community colleges, of which we were one, but when it came to
universities it was a totally new situation. The University of Jordan
had been established by royal decree and was not under the Jordanian Ministry of Education. Israeli universities were quite independent, yet the military authorities in the occupied territories wanted
us to be completely under their control.

In the end, we just filled in a simple form, telling the Israelis how
many students we were anticipating, our areas of specialisation and
so on. Based on this, we applied for and were duly issued a military government permit. What it stated was that we were allowed
to function for the academic year 1972/73, but would have to
apply again the following year if we wanted to continue. We were
less than thrilled with the short period covered by the permit. Our
university was not like a liquor store which can operate this year
and not the next. Still, we had brought it off – to a limited extent.

Eventually, when we had our first graduation in June 1976, I
wrote a letter to the military governor, telling him that we were now
a university with permanent buildings that constituted a significant
investment. We had students that were with us long-term and thus
regarded the permit we had as a permanent one. We would not be
applying again for a renewal. We never received a reply, but we felt
we had established yet another fact on the ground and asserted our
rights.

On the same principle, we tried to give the military as little
information as possible, being especially careful not to volunteer
any of it. For example, we never passed on the addresses of our
students beyond the name of their home town or village. This
greatly annoyed the military governor, but we insisted that was all
we knew. The Israelis came to realise that we would comply with
what was absolutely necessary, but would not go any further.

Whenever we were asked to attend a meeting, our president,
Hanna Nasir, and I would go together, as the Israelis might find it
easier to intimidate one man alone. We tried to establish a pattern

whereby the Israelis would not order us around but would respect us and treat us in a professional manner, even if they did not like the idea.

The Israelis, we concluded, had been caught unawares by our founding a university, having thought us incapable of such a feat. However, the obstacles we encountered once Birzeit University existed quickly showed us just how unenthusiastic they really were about it.

The first problem arose over a plot of land in Ramallah we had bought in 1969 through an agreement with the Municipality of Ramallah in the name of Birzeit College, to be the site of the new campus of the university. The reason for our choice of site was the greater accessibility of Ramallah to all parts of the occupied territories as well as the presence of developed infrastructure for building a campus. At that time the land registry office was not operational, and so our agreement was just between the college and the municipality. Later, the military government refused to recognise the university's ownership because its board was not yet registered, and so the Mayor of Ramallah asked the military governor for the plot to be expropriated for the public good. This too was rejected. This left us with a loss, as the price of the purchase had been 10,000 Jordanian dinars, a huge sum in those days. Moreover, we had already paid a surveyor for a site plan and an architect to design the first building.

Our default action was to seek permission to build on another stretch of land already owned by the university. This was situated on the road between Birzeit and Ramallah and consisted of a patchwork of agricultural plots. As traditional practices of inheritance led to large pieces of land being divided into multiple plots, it had taken us years to purchase all of these from their owners, some of whom now lived abroad. The next stage, a necessary change in the zoning category from agricultural land to building land, should have taken two months at the most. The military government dragged it out over two years.

Even more obstructive was the military government's attitude to books. As soon as the university started out, its officers demanded copies of all the textbooks we were using. Most of the books were in English and had been published in the United States or Britain. As they had been expensive, we told the military: 'We will give you a list of their titles and you can then get them.' They firmly rejected this and insisted on being given our copies.

'OK,' we said. 'We'll let you have the books for inspection, but you must give them back as soon as you are through with them.'

The outcome was rather different. After two months, we asked the military for the return of our books. Alternatively, we said, they ought to pay for them. Our letters about this went unanswered. Several more months passed, but eventually we managed to get our way. Having received a letter from the education officer in the military government in which he asked us for information about our students, I responded by writing: 'I will not answer your letter until you answer all of mine.' I then listed the dates on which these had been sent.

Two days later, I received a letter from the officer, saying 'Please come and collect your books.' It was a victory of sorts, though not a lasting one.

As time went by, the military government became increasingly obsessed with our reading lists. Books we ordered from abroad were often permanently confiscated without us even setting our eyes on them. Among those banned were works on archaeology and history, as well as several journals on Arabic literature. These included *Al-Aadab* and *Al-Adeeb,* two cultural journals published in Lebanon, and *Majallet Ad-Drirasat al Filisteeniyyah (Journal of Palestine Studies)*, a sociopolitical journal published in Kuwait. All were freely available to students at Israeli universities.

Yet another obstructive technique was to impose huge taxes on imported teaching materials. In the early 1980s we ordered a small mainframe computer, probably the first of its kind to be used in the West Bank for education purposes. It cost around $50,000 and the Israelis demanded almost the same amount again in taxes and duties, which was crippling for us. Israeli universities could of course reclaim such costs, while Birzeit could not.

Perhaps the most destructive intervention was the denial of residence permits to our international staff. Nearly all of them had, by necessity, been educated abroad, and among them were not just Palestinians returning to their homeland but also citizens of the United States, Britain, France and a range of other countries.

These academics were renowned subject specialists who enabled us to develop the syllabus as well to offer a wider range of courses. It was also a matter of policy for us to let students experience a variety of different outlooks. The presence of the international staff also had an irritant effect on the Israeli military. As outside observers, they could describe the human rights violations they observed to people in their own countries, where they were seen by the media as more trustworthy than we were, as mere natives. Their presence also offered us a chance to link up with the academic fraternity

Ground-breaking of the new campus, 1976

abroad. All this was greatly valued by us, but a thorn in the side of the military.

One of the officers who was keenest to get rid of the inconvenient outsiders was the military governor of the West Bank in the mid-1970s, Binyamin Ben Eliezer. Known as 'Fuad' among fellow Israelis because he was a Jew from Iraq, he spoke fluent Arabic and behaved in a friendly manner whenever we met. However, he also made it increasingly hard for foreign academics to remain legally in Birzeit. Lecturers' residence permits were not renewed, and those who went home for the holidays could sometimes not get back in. Since foreigners constituted at that point around a third of our academic staff, such measures were extremely disruptive to the education process.

To make up for this, Fuad offered us a deal. He would issue a few of the precious 'family reunification' visas to Palestinian academics abroad, so they could teach at Birzeit instead. When I told him that I could name, off-hand, at least four of our academics keen to get back, he advised us to apply. In the event, only two such applications were approved. Fuad, however, retained his reputation (at least outside the West Bank) as a liberal figure. He held the housing portfolio in the Rabin government of 1992–94, and was then appointed leader of the Israeli Labour Party. In 2001, he joined Ariel Sharon's coalition government and became its defence minister.

Despite the obstacles put in our path, all of us at Birzeit were determined to turn the university into a haven of excellence, fairness and democracy. For a start, admission was by merit alone. Students were given a place purely on the strength of their matriculation grades, irrespective of family background or ability to pay. Once accepted, an applicant could ask to be exempted from tuition fees altogether, request a reduction or obtain a loan. A committee that included students would then scrutinise the applications and visit the students at home to check they were indeed poor. This admissions process brought in lots of bright young students from disadvantaged communities, a group which had hitherto stood no chance of entering higher education. Many would go on to have impressive careers.

Religious affiliation was not allowed to play a role in the admissions process either. We did not even ask applicants what their religion was, a policy quite unheard of in our region. All that mattered was ability.

Even the considerable variation among teaching standards within West Bank schools was not allowed to affect the outcome. Birzeit tested applicants for their grasp of science and English, but offered bridging courses to those in need. I gave my own classes in biology and chemistry at 8 am each day, so I could keep an eye on general progress.

The student mix we were faced with on the first day of our new degree course reflected our ideals. Streaming into our lecture halls were young people from all backgrounds and from all over: there were modern girls in short skirts from the cities and village girls in long dresses, boys from middle-class homes in new, good-quality shirts and trousers, and boys from refugee camps in faded but carefully ironed clothes. Some had smart watches. Others had never owned one.

The university education for this very diverse intake was designed to be as broad as possible. Science students had to also take some arts subjects in their first year. Students of the humanities were obliged to study one unit of science.

Young people arriving at Birzeit found themselves not just preparing for a degree but also engaging with wider questions. As the West Bank's school syllabus was rather narrow, each of our students had to attend four courses on the intellectual history of mankind through the ages. This would start with the Greeks, then move from Locke, Hobbs, Hume and Marx to Ghassan Kanafani, a leading Palestinian literary figure, assassinated by the Israelis in 1972. Students would read Dante's *Divine Comedy*, stage Shakespeare plays and listen to music from a variety of countries. A cultural studies course was designed to narrow the gap between students of very different family backgrounds. On outings, they would discuss ethical questions with their lecturers in both English and Arabic.

Since we felt certain we would have a state of our own very soon, we also emphasised the importance of democracy. Students learnt to value freedom of speech, but also that this did not mean you could insult or libel people. There had to be limits. Students had a chance to practise democracy in the students union. Everybody there had a right to be listened to, there were free elections and, while factions did gradually form, they had to resolve their differences by nonviolent means. At Birzeit, there would be no fights and no weapons. Disagreements had to be resolved by dialogue.

When asked to give my own opinion, I always did, but made sure that it was presented as one of several possible views. I would also accept valid criticism from the student union over administrative issues, something quite new in our society.

Observing democratic principles could lead to uncomfortable situations. One day, the student union held a protest against a price rise imposed by the university cafeteria, calling on everyone to boycott it. When I arrived for my lunch, my path was blocked by a rather short girl called Ilham Khoury, who told me that I could not enter as this would be a breach of the student union's resolution. I hesitated for a moment, but then nodded and turned back. The girl looked absolutely stunned. Her fellow students later told me that they had much appreciated my lesson in democracy.

At the same time, students were expected to take on duties. Student reps would sit on the university's admissions committee, financial committee and even academic council, required to absorb information and to share responsibility for decisions.

An even more important part of Birzeit's education process was its voluntary work programme. During their course, students had to spend 120 hours working in the community. Youngsters who had never even been inside an ordinary village would dig drainage ditches in refugee camps, weed fields or help with the olive harvest. Since a good proportion of our students came from the economic

The author addressing students in the old campus, 1975

elite (as even senior school was too costly for many Palestinians), it was a way of encouraging humility and of bringing our social classes together. It was also an opportunity for the students to make fun of me: being 6ft 4, I was the only person not to need a ladder when we went olive picking.

Thus the university became, for a while at least, an oasis of democratic freedom in the occupied territories. Outside it, though, people's quality of life was rapidly deteriorating. Educated Palestinians who had been employed in the administrative sector under the Jordanians found that the Israeli military personnel were now administering the West Bank. Confiscations continued, not just of farmland but also of Palestinian homes in what the Israeli army deemed to be strategic locations. Houses were emptied, shops sealed shut.

Early most mornings, we would see clusters of dejected Palestinians gather at highway junctions and wait for the pick-up trucks of Israeli farmers or factory owners. Burly men would descend and, after some bargaining, offer work to the strongest looking and those offering to work for the lowest wages. Palestinians from the occupied territories were not officially allowed to sleep in pre-1967 Israel, so these labourers either had to make the long journey both ways twice a day, or stay over illegally, sleeping in Israeli sheds, fields or old air-raid shelters. Anyone who was caught could expect a prison sentence and a hefty fine. Employers often took advantage of the men's powerlessness, making them work 16 hours a day and sometimes beating them.

Meanwhile, our Gaza students arrived with terrible tales. The Gaza Strip was now administered by General Ariel Sharon. Faced with a huge population of actively hostile Palestinian refugees, Sharon and his paratrooper units had unleashed a reign of terror. Hundreds of hovels belonging to these dispossessed, wretchedly poor people were bulldozed. Soldiers stormed into every house, seizing men and boys and making them stand outside for identity parades often lasting all night. Anyone suspected of resistance activities was shot on sight. Altogether, well over a thousand people had died in this way by 1972.

Initially, my family seemed sheltered from all this. Haifa and I now lived in a large house on a hill just outside Ramallah, together with a gradually expanded family of three small children. Our new home, which was the first to be built on this quiet spot, had a separate wing for my parents and a large, pleasant sitting room directly accessible from the front door. This door was always open and students and staff would frequently drop by. On St Barbara's Day, when the university was still small we would invite the faculty and staff to our house to share with us the traditional special sweet dish of wheat, raisins and sugar that Haifa usually prepares on this occasion.

From our windows, guests had a beautiful view right across the plains and valleys of occupied Palestine. Looking out, people would sometimes burst into one of the poet Kamal Nasser's popular songs:

Oh, my brother the refugee,
Live and do not despair
For adversity revives those with dignified spirit.
You must yet return and forever
To the plains of Jaffa and the hills of Jerusalem.
Behold, the shores of Palestine are anxious for you,
Its farmland is longing for your hands to till.
The curse of generations will stay upon you
If you forget the holy city of Jerusalem.

One fine spring Sunday, Haifa decided to take the children for a walk through some wild meadows nearby. Just as during my childhood, every inch of soil was covered with wild flowers such as narcissi and tulips, and she thought they would enjoy picking a couple of bunches. The children ran here and there, excited by the bright colours. Within minutes, a soldier holding a machine gun appeared from nowhere and walked up to their little group, asking sharply: 'What are you doing there?'

Haifa replied that they were just taking some fresh air, but the soldier, towering over them, was not satisfied. Where had they come from, he asked. Nervously, Haifa pointed to their nearby house. 'Hurry up, get away, then,' shouted the soldier. 'You can't be on these hills without a permit.' Clutching her terrified children, Haifa quickly walked back home.

Although none of them had come to any actual harm, the incident suggested that nothing belonged to Palestinians any more. Even common land was now state land – land that belonged to the Israeli state, that is. So Haifa never took the risk of going on this kind of harmless Sunday walk again. The children too seemed traumatised by their encounter with the military. Little did they know that far worse was in store.

4

TARGETING BIRZEIT

The Israelis struck their first serious blow against Birzeit University just after the October 1973 (Yom Kippur) war. It was a tense time with an increased military presence in the West Bank. Now, many of the Israeli soldiers seemed to be older than before. Curfews were imposed that seemed to go on forever.

One of our former students, today working for a major NGO, still recalls the dilemma which this punitive measure created for him. As a refugee camp dweller, he found himself confined to the boundaries of his camp at a time when he needed to sit his school matriculation finals outside it. Curfew-breakers risked getting shot and his family advised him against leaving. But he had worked hard for this exam and was keen to continue to university. So he decided to get up before dawn, when he figured there would be little military presence in the streets, and run for it. He had miscalculated, it turned out, and ended up being chased by a group of soldiers, guns cocked, towards Ramallah and the examination hall. Only because he was young and could run extremely fast did he arrive there in one piece.

By then, Birzeit had been the site of non-violent protests for several years. Students affected by the land confiscations and other repressive measures would march back and forth, shouting slogans in which they demanded freedom from the occupation. It was our campus, a Palestinian campus, and so we allowed this. The military government pretended not to understand the logic of this. Officers kept turning up at our university offices, advising Hanna and me to keep our noses clean, ordering us to stop the students from causing trouble. We explained that Birzeit was a university, not an infant school; we could not be held responsible for everything the students did.

Soon after, a group of students went on a silent demonstration in Ramallah, all of them wearing black, to protest against the occupation. The army swooped down on them with full force and

30 students were arrested. Each was offered the choice of paying a fine of between 100 and 300 Jordanian dinars or being kept in jail. These were 18-year-old boys and girls, and their parents, many of them penniless refugees, came to us for help. As the military would not relent, we had to run a fundraising drive to cover the fines, so that everyone was freed.

Unfortunately, one day in December 1973, just before the university's Christmas break, the outcome of student protests was more serious for the university. There had been yet another student demonstration consisting of the usual 'march around Jericho' on campus territory. The army had rushed in and broken it up by beating any student they could get hold of, as they had done many times before.

Still, the problem seemed to be over. A couple of days later, though, Hanna Nasir telephoned me and said, 'Gabi, you know what has happened? They have closed the college.' It was shocking, something we had never anticipated, the closing of a major educational institution.

'What do you mean, they've closed the college?' I said.

'We have an order from the military governor that we should close the college for an "indefinite" period of time,' Hanna replied.

'What should we do? We have boarders; where should they go?' I said.

I went immediately to Birzeit to see him and we held an emergency 'kitchen cabinet' with our academic staff. What was most urgent was to make arrangements for the students to be taken home in local buses.

We were all reeling from the day's events. Birzeit had been established as an institution for the Palestinian people. It was looked upon with pride as a national institution. By this I do not mean that it was a centre for nationalism or for opposition to the Israelis. It was simply a place where our people could at last enjoy the blessings of higher education. Seeing it closed down was a bitter blow to the Palestinian consciousness.

We spent endless hours discussing what could be done. The chairman of our board of trustees at the time was Bishop Qub'ain, an elderly man who was very well respected, having been the first Arab bishop of the Anglican Church in Palestine. We asked him to intervene on our behalf. We also decided to mobilise public support by writing newspaper articles and talking to journalists. This was a new form of activity for most of us. Communicating with the media, and especially its international representatives, took time, patience and a thick skin. However, we wanted people everywhere to know about what was happening to our university and we needed their support.

As we explained the Palestinians' right to higher education and how we were fulfilling this, we were amazed to find that reporters and even editors often hardly knew we existed, except as obstacles to the project of creating a large, powerful Jewish state. Even journalists who had travelled widely sometimes found it hard to grasp that a people, the Palestinians, had lived in this country for the last 2,000 years, had planted crops, created exquisite buildings and gradually developed the same aspirations as other peoples, including that of possessing a national university. Jews had been allowed by the British to create theirs, the Hebrew University of Jerusalem, in 1925, but it was assumed that Palestinians could do without.

Foreigners, we discovered, were taken around by Israeli tour guides who only told them about Jewish history and Israeli achievements. Our people were described by them as essentially nomadic, without attachment to the land and without aspirations. Our protests against expulsion or repression were attributed to the inherently quarrelsome nature of something called 'the Arab mind'.

We were up against a determined and sophisticated propaganda machine. The *Jerusalem Post*, Israel's main English language paper, which is widely read abroad, published a flood of letters which dismissed Birzeit as a mere centre for Palestinian nationalism. Israeli politicians argued that we were just peddling anti-Israeli sentiments. In response, our message to the public was: we are not anti-Israeli, we are pro-Palestinian. The Palestinian people were human beings and so they had rights too. These included the right to an education.

As a result, some observers began to develop an interest in and sympathy for Birzeit. Partly because of this, the military government changed its stand. Grudgingly, it allowed the university to reopen after only two weeks. Still, its closure had set a most unfortunate precedent. This was the first of 15 military-ordered closures of the university, ranging in duration from two weeks to three months, prior to the long closure during the first intifada which lasted 51 months.

The next stage in Israel's hostility to Birzeit was the harassment of Israeli Arab lecturers and students at the university. These people were citizens of Israel, but also Palestinians like us. I had first met

some of them when they'd come over to visit us during the main
Greek Orthodox feasts, Christmas and Easter. My brother George
had an Israeli Arab friend whom he'd met when both were studying in Turkey, and when that man had come to stay with us he
had told us about the discrimination his community was suffering.
Its members were under constant police surveillance, harassed by
members of the public and denied most of the welfare benefits
and economic aid enjoyed by Israeli Jews. Their homes were badly
overcrowded and their schools crumbling from lack of funds. Other
Palestinian visitors had helped to fill out this dismal picture with
similar accounts.

So when the military authorities asked: 'Why do you have these
Israeli students at the university?' we knew enough to answer: 'First
of all, Palestinians living inside Israel have little chance to go to
Israeli universities.' It was easy enough to prove this at the time.
In 1967, Israeli Arabs constituted something like 15 per cent of
the Israeli population, but less than half a per cent of the country's
university population.

'Secondly,' we went on, 'Palestinians living inside Israel and those
living in the West Bank are from the same stock. We in the West
Bank are no more intelligent than they are. So, how come so many
of us had a university education, yet so few of them had?' The
Israeli officer did not attempt to answer, but insisted that we had to
remove the Israeli Arab students from the university. I kept arguing
about it and finished up telling him that if he really wanted us to get
the students out of Birzeit he should serve us with a military order.
He said, 'Okay, I'll give you the order.'

I never got an actual order, but the Israelis began to harass these
students and faculty. Questions were even asked in the Knesset (the
Israeli parliament) as to why these Israeli Arabs were studying at
Birzeit, which was alleged to be a centre for anti-Israeli sentiments.
The Minister of Defence was Shimon Peres at that time, and we
put an open letter in the *Jerusalem Post* answering these charges.
Some Israeli Arab members of the Knesset also defended the right
of Israeli Arabs to join Birzeit.

We noticed that the Israeli media were not finding it easy to
justify such repressive measures. After all, Israelis had up to this
point claimed to be conducting what they described as an 'enlightened' or 'benevolent' occupation. They wanted the world to believe
that they supported academic freedom, because they knew that
many people, including Jews living in other countries, held this in
the highest regard. Jews had traditionally been extremely education

oriented, and even we ourselves had never dreamt that they might take such anti-education steps.

To regain the lost ground, the mainstream Israeli daily *Yediot Ahronot* published an article that went back into the history of Birzeit in the 1930s and 1940s, telling its readers that the institution was even then known to be encouraging Arab nationalism. That part of it was true and we were not ashamed of it. What to us was 'nationalistic' was 'criminal' to them, because they could see anything we did only as anti-Israeli. They never thought of Palestinians as neighbours or fellow countrymen and did not want anyone to know that they had stolen a land from another people.

However, once people started to talk about Palestinian or Arab nationalism, Israelis were forced to explain why there was a nation and that there had been people living for centuries in this so-called 'land without a people for a people without a land'. We, the Palestinians, were not supposed to have any Palestinian national feeling, as we were painted as just a part of the Arab world. In fact, we were not supposed to exist.

To distract from the inconvenient truth, Israelis made all sorts of untrue claims. Some commentators insisted that we were still a high school. Others said that Birzeit had been established for the sole purpose of agitating against the Israeli occupation. Our nation's need for higher education meant nothing to Israelis. It was as if we had nothing on our minds apart from upsetting Israel.

To this day, Israelis, it seems, can only perceive us in the negative. To them, we are not Palestinians, we are 'non-Jews', the phrase used during the early years of the British mandate to describe 90 per cent of the population of Palestine.

It seems that by our very existence as a Palestinian institution we are 'inciting hostility against Israel'. Anything that is positive for our own people is automatically viewed as negative for Israel. If something good is being done for the Palestinians, it must by definition be bad for the Israelis. Producing a generation of better-educated Palestinians was seen as threatening by Israel and clearly we had to be closed down or stopped.

Successive Israeli governments are guilty of conducting a huge, never-ending campaign of misinformation directed at their own people. Most Israelis have no direct knowledge of the former inhabitants of the land they now inhabit. The brainwashing which they have undergone about the history, society and culture of the Palestinians has done enormous damage, as well as making it increasingly difficult for our two nations to be reconciled.

On 20 November 1974, Hanna Nasir was summoned to the
offices of the military governor and, as usual, I decided to come
along. It was a time of great public agitation. A few days earlier,
Yasser Arafat had addressed the United Nations for the first time
ever, as its General Assembly was about to pass Resolution 3236,
affirming the PLO as 'the representative of the Palestinian people'.
Palestinians interpreted this as an acknowledgement by the international community of the case for Palestinian nationhood and
Palestinian rights. People had been demonstrating in the streets, but
for once to express their joy rather than to protest.

The next day, the students at Birzeit had conducted their usual
'walk around Jericho', but their mood now was darker because
they had just heard that in Nablus a young woman demonstrator
had been shot dead. Soon, Israeli soldiers turned up and, yet again,
there was violence, directed by the soldiers at the students. The situation escalated, and when Hanna saw that the soldiers were about
to open fire he tried to calm them down by saying: 'These students
are my responsibility. If you fire one bullet there will be a bloodbath
here, because they will throw stones back at you.' He promised to
lead the students back into the campus, which he did.

You would have thought that this was a good deed, but we now
discovered that our uniformed rulers felt differently. The military
governor, so Hanna told me, had demanded to see him at 11 pm
that night. That sounded very strange. While the Israelis had previously called us late in the evening, they had never done so this late.
'Be ready, I'll pick you up on my way,' Hanna told me. Usually, he
tried to arrive early so that we could talk for a bit before we went
on.

When it was nearly 11 pm and Hanna still wasn't there, I
decided to drive to Birzeit with Haifa, thinking, 'Maybe something
happened to him on the way.' In fact Hanna, who was travelling
with his mother and Wadi' Nasir, had been delayed at an army
checkpoint near Surda. Once he was through the checkpoint, we
decided we would all accompany him to the military governor's
office.

As we rushed though the gate towards the governor's headquarters, the Muqata'a, an officer called Captain Maurice (later
promoted to Major) blocked our way. Only Hanna, he said, was
allowed in. 'I want to go with him as I usually do,' I told the
Captain. 'There's no need,' he replied. 'This time everything will be
okay.'

According to Captain Maurice, Hanna had simply been asked

to attend a meeting with the local mayors to discuss education and suchlike. This sounded rather strange, so I told the officer I would wait outside. Just before setting off, Hanna turned to us and simply said, 'I'll see you later.' These were the last words we were to hear from him for a long time.

Meanwhile, the rest of us settled down in our car. Captain Maurice tried to tell us that we did not need to wait, but we insisted. After a while, we returned to the gate and Captain Maurice came out to speak to us. 'It's getting very late and we don't know what's happening,' I told him. He replied that Hanna was still in that meeting, so I explained that I had Hanna's car keys and asked him to pass them on to him. We left his car outside the Muqata'a

We all then went to my home in my car and waited until 3 o'clock in the morning. It was now both raining and cold but Haifa and I decided to return to the Muqata'a. The gate was closed and the whole building was silent, with all the lights turned off. We banged on the gate for a while but nobody responded and there was no way for us to get in. I advised Mrs Nasir, Hanna's mother, to go home with Wadi', while I would stay on. However, they both decided against this and we dozed a little in our respective cars for some time before making our way back.

In the Nasir family's home, Hanna's wife Tania was frantic. She had been suspicious of this summons from the beginning, but was unable to accompany him as she had a sick child and two infants. As he left, she had noticed that the temperature had dropped and told him: 'Please, take your sports jacket; this will end late and you might be cold.'

At dawn, when Hanna was still not back, Tania phoned to ask me what to do. I advised her to start contacting the international journalists we knew.

When I walked into Birzeit that morning, the atmosphere was extremely tense. Armed soldiers were milling about for no obvious reason. At around 8 o'clock I called the military governor, Colonel Feldman, directly, and asked him: 'What's happening? If you have arrested Dr Nasir, you should have told us.' He insisted that he knew nothing about any arrest but would check it out. 'Please do so,' I said, 'because we want to know what the problem is. Dr Nasir might require a lawyer.'

At around 8.30 am, the students sensed that something was wrong and refused to go into classes. At this point, the army surrounded the university. A few minutes later, some students came up and told me that they had seen soldiers march into the campus from the back. I rushed out there and shouted at the soldiers, telling them to get out. To my utter amazement, they did. None of them argued, they just left.

Just outside the gate nearest to the library, I saw an officer and some soldiers chasing a group of students. I shouted at them, 'Don't you dare come in here! You are not allowed in!' The officer looked at me for a moment, then told the soldiers to stay out. But they still hung around just outside the walls of the campus.

It was a worrying situation, yet all we could do was wait. We asked the students to calm down and I rang the military governor again about Hanna's fate. He said he would look into the matter. We went into our classes, but broke at 10 am to listen to the news. Tania had heard an Israeli newscaster broadcasting in Hebrew mention Hanna's name a little earlier. She thought he might be in jail. We now learned from the radio that deportation orders had been served on Hanna Nasir and four others. All four were being deported to South Lebanon.

With one stroke of the military pen, our university had been deprived of its president. You can imagine how we felt. It was a huge blow to us all. I cannot describe my feeling at that moment. Not only was this act illegal and counter to international law and the 4th Geneva Convention, but it was also immoral and sadistic. To uproot a person from his country, society and family and simply throw him across the border of another country against the wishes of that country is beyond my understanding.

It now became obvious why the army had surrounded the campus. As we sat there in deep shock, all I could think of was Hanna turning to us the night before, as he went in to the military governor's office and saying, 'I'll see you later.'

The students immediately went on strike and began to demonstrate inside the campus. However, as the army was surrounding it, there was not much that either of the parties could do.

Our academic staff mobilised and protested to the authorities. We also tried to alert friends of Birzeit University abroad, but we did not know where Hanna was, or even if he was inside or outside the country. Later we learned from a Lebanese radio station that the deportees were already in Lebanon. It was a shocking outcome. Hanna's youngest child, a baby girl of just under a year, his wife and the rest of his family were left in the West Bank. He had not even been allowed to say goodbye.

At that time Israel did not allow us phone lines to the Arab world, so there was no way of calling to find out what exactly had happened to Hanna or how he was. It was not until much later that we developed 'illicit' systems of communication between ourselves and the Arab world.

We first heard from Hanna about a week after his deportation, through the International Red Cross. He was in Beirut and told us that on the night of his deportation he had been put in a room and read a statement announcing that he was to be deported. He was then handcuffed, blindfolded and taken to a vehicle that he later realised was a jeep. Once inside it, he realised that there were other Palestinians there and he said, 'I am Hanna Nasir.' The soldiers ordered him to shut up. However, another voice replied: 'You too, Hanna?' It was his friend, Alfred Toubasi, a dentist. It gave him some comfort that he was not alone.

There were four prisoners in the jeep. A fifth deportee, it later turned out, was the contractor Abdel Razzak Odeh, who was flown by helicopter to their destination, Al Naqura on the Lebanese border, on the morning of 21 November.

First, though, the men were driven around for hours, unable to work out the direction. Hanna later revealed that this was the worst part as they did not know what to expect and as the blindfolds were painfully tight. Eventually, they were told to get off the jeep, allowed to look around and told by the Israeli soldiers to keep walking. 'If you try to come back,' they said, 'we are going to shoot you.'

South Lebanon was known as 'Fateh Land' because it was full of Palestinian refugee camps and controlled by the PLO, of which Fateh was the largest faction. So the men followed the road until they were met by a Lebanese border patrol, which instantly arrested them. As the deportees looked pretty dishevelled, the patrolmen suspected that they were trying to enter illegally and took them to their office. There they were questioned roughly, as the Israelis had taken away their identity documents, making it impossible for them to prove who they were. Fortunately, there was a radio in the room and when a patrolman decided to listen to the BBC Arabic Service, he heard its London newsreader announce: 'This morning, five distinguished leading figures from Palestine were deported.' This changed the attitude of the Lebanese.

In the days after the deportation, we approached various foreign consulates to see if they could help in any way. None did. Also, every time I met with the military governor, I would bring up the matter of Hanna's deportation. As time went by, we took to sending protest letters at the beginning of each year, asking for the rescinding of the order and Hanna's return. His mother applied to Israel for a family reunion visa for him, which was denied. Occasionally we would get a form letter saying something like, 'We have received your letter and we are unable to meet your request.'

We pressed on with our protests because we felt we had a good case. Hanna was in no way a violent person and did not belong to any of the Palestinian factions. He had simply been doing his duty as president of the university. Still, the Israelis did not allow him to appeal. In fact, in those days deportees were never given an opportunity to plead to the Israeli High Court of Justice. Nor were they told the reasons for their deportation. Can you imagine what it is like to be suddenly torn from your family, your home, your country and expelled to a foreign land without even knowing why?

When Hanna's case started to receive media attention, Israeli politicians began to say that he had been 'inciting students' and other such baloney. On the Israeli radio there were reports that he had been inciting people to demonstrate and riot (see Appendix II: Deportation).

The Israelis refused to acknowledge that the man they had expelled was a top educator. He was not just the president of the West Bank's first university, but also a reputable physicist and a very popular lecturer in his subject.

I saw Hanna again for the first time after his deportation in February 1975, while he was still in Beirut. It was not easy for us to leave the West Bank then, and when I went abroad I needed the permission of the military governor. Every time from then onwards, he would specifically instruct me, 'You are not to meet with Hanna Nasir.' I was not planning to tell him if I did.

Israel's excuses for the deportation gradually changed. Years later, when Hanna joined the PLO Executive Committee, the Israelis would answer any letters of protest about his deportation with the assertion that he had been deported because he was 'an Executive Committee member of the Palestine Liberation Organisation, a terrorist organisation that seeks the destruction of the State of Israel'. The fact that he had only joined the Executive Committee six years after his deportation did not bother them. They would tell this lie to justify their action to the outside world and, unfortunately, many people believed it. When faced with human rights violations of this scale, many will simply ask themselves: 'Why would a government deport law-abiding citizens? Surely they must have done something.'

What people should ask is: 'Why did they not put this person on trial, present evidence against him and put him in jail?' Deportation is a convenient way of getting rid of people who are in your way without going through the inconvenience of due legal process. Israel's military occupation is, in part, held in place by the common excuse of 'security reasons'. This phrase works like a key when it comes to spiriting the accused into custody or deportation by the back door without the proper process of a trial. It justifies extra-legal procedures with reference to the need to preserve the secrecy of intelligence information.

Sometimes, of course, there is no such information at all. The fact was, Hanna Nasir was head of the largest independent Palestinian national institution in the occupied territories. This was enough of a crime in the eyes of a state which had lied for so many years to the world and to its own immigrants about this being 'a land without a people for a people without a land'.

Hanna's was merely one of many deportations. The mayors of Ramallah and Al-Bireh, who were both very active in working for their cities, suffered the same fate. They too were part of something that Israel was determined to nip in the bud, something that by its very existence disproved the lie of the empty land. For that reason, they deserved deportation.

By now, Israel has deported well over 1,500 people. It remains a way of making examples of prominent Palestinian leaders and of punishing ordinary political activists who have not committed any violent acts. The deportations of such people serve as a warning to others not to do anything 'wrong'.

Although measures were subsequently introduced which required reasons to be given for a deportation and ensured that a detainee had access to the Israeli High Court, I am not aware of any case in which that Court reversed a deportation order before someone was deported. Most people refused to appeal, as they realised that any negative decision by the High Court would make it more difficult for them to come back later.

At that time, deportation was used more than detention, which gives some idea of the political climate in those days. Yet Israel's use of detention was similar to its use of deportation in that it observed no due process of law. There were no other levels of court in this system, which made appeals pointless. The establishment of military courts on 7 June 1967 had been one of the first actions of the Israeli government after the occupation of the West Bank and Gaza Strip.

Israel was on the defensive at that time, making all sorts of

excuses for its behaviour. Nonetheless, after Hanna's deportation
the international media started to take a greater interest in its
human rights record. Britain's *Sunday Times* ran a series of articles
on detention and detainees in an exposé which highlighted Israel's
extensive use of measures against individuals without any due
process of law. Sadly, such reports did not stop the practice.

For Hanna's family, the deportation created ongoing problems.
Tania, his wife, was left on her own for the first three months,
as she and Hanna had shared an identity document and without
it she was not allowed to leave the country. When she eventually obtained the military governor's permission to do so, she
was harassed mercilessly at the Israeli border crossing points by
the Jordan river. The crossing was dreaded by all Palestinians,
because they often had to queue for eight hours without food or
water for the children. Tania, though, was singled out each time
for especially harsh treatment.

Once, when she had left her home at 3 am with the children in
order to get to the bridge by car, the Israeli border guard took one
look at her travel document and said: 'Sorry, you can't cross. Only
the children can.'

'What do you mean?' Tania said. 'They can't go without me! The
eldest is nine years old and the youngest is a baby!'

He was totally unmoved and went on to tell her: 'If you feel that
way, go back to the military governor and take it up with him!'
Tania had to return home, find a lawyer and take her case to the
Israeli courts. She was eventually allowed through, but the process
took several weeks. It was obvious that she had been singled out for
harassment.

What was even more distressing about the crossing were the
strip searches. The soldiers at the bridge would look through everything. They even strip-searched the children, looking through their
nappies. As Tania later told a reporter:

> My children grew up on that bridge. One of my kids had
> already said emotional goodbyes to his grandparents and we
> were on our way to the border crossing, when the driver of
> our cab got into an argument with a soldier. The argument
> became progressively nastier and my son became hysterical.
> He had a crying fit and kept saying: 'I'm scared, I'm scared,
> please stop!' So we had to go back, past those endless rows
> of waiting cars, until he was better and we could find another
> driver, so we could cross at last. He was only four years old.

People don't realise how much such small incidents can affect children.

Witnessing the effects of deportation on such close friends of mine led me to draw some important conclusions. Banishing someone from his or her own country is, I believe, one of the cruellest measures that can be used against a person. What made it particularly cruel was that Hanna was closely connected to an institution. He was not an ordinary teacher who could happily work anywhere. He was deeply involved in Birzeit's development at a time when it was just taking off and beginning to develop into a fully fledged university. There was no clearer sign of Israel's contempt for Palestinian efforts to improve educational standards among their people.

When we realised Hanna was not likely to come back soon, Birzeit's academic staff and students discussed the future. We all agreed that he would remain our president, wherever he was. I would officially continue as his deputy, but I carried all presidential duties pertaining to the daily management of the university and would take necessary presidential decisions, in consultation with him.

The horror of what happened to Hanna never ceased to worry me whenever I was called to the military governor's office, especially in the evenings. I was always afraid that the same could happen to me. I took precautions such as seeking legal counsel and discovered that when you are arrested you can get your lawyer to put in a request to the Israeli High Court of Justice to suspend legal proceedings until reasons are given for the deportation. Sadly, this procedure only has the effect of delaying the deportation and not of cancelling it. Our lawyer at the time was Elias Khoury, who had already gained much experience in this field. I instructed him to take action on my behalf if anything like this should happen again. Fortunately, it never did and I am grateful for that.

Nor, however, did the military government ever slacken its efforts to deprive the university of its academic staff in various ways. Almost every one of our lecturers has been held by the military for some length of time. In most cases it is just a day or two, but Tayseer Arouri, an instructor of physics at Birzeit, was detained in 1974 and held in a 6-metre by 8-metre room with 63 people for two years. Only when a Red Cross mission visited the jail and issued a highly critical report were conditions improved. When we asked the military governor to give a reason for his detention, his response was: 'We think he was thinking of doing something.'

Tayseer was never charged with any offence, but was held for 45 months altogether – almost four years – through the use of repeatedly renewed administrative detention orders. The first order had been for three months, and then the rest were for six months at a time, making his the longest detention period to date. Altogether, Tayseer's detention order was renewed seven separate times.

What made these measures possible was Israeli Military Order 378, which allows the military judge to issue an order extending detention and prohibits access to lawyers for a maximum of 90 days. The order can be renewed over a period of several years.

A few years later Marwan Awartani, our Professor of Mathematics and a new father, was arrested during a visit to Nablus. He was not charged with anything, nor did he go through any legal process, but was kept in solitary confinement for a total of 17 months. During that time, he was denied books, newspapers, study materials, visits and private conversations with his lawyer. Amnesty International has defined solitary confinement as a form of torture, a cruel, severe and often permanently damaging violation of human rights. It is the kind of prisoner treatment only the worst of regimes use.

The military government also had no hesitation in endangering academics' lives. Hanan Ashrawi remembers a particularly shocking event from her university days:

> When I was head of Birzeit's English department and nine months pregnant, the Israelis besieged the university. I tried to negotiate with them, so that they would lift the siege and let our students get home, but they were not interested. Instead, the soldiers let fly, not just with teargas but with bullets. Together with another female lecturer, both of us pregnant, I ended up hiding under a table, trying to dodge the bullets while the teargas was blinding us. They had no respect for anyone or anything.

5

DEVELOPING BIRZEIT

In the light of these concerted efforts to suppress Palestinian attempts to provide quality higher education for its young people, it almost defies belief that Israel went on to claim credit for the development of Palestinian higher education. Having seen Birzeit withstand the first wave of Israeli pressure, several other colleges followed our example in upgrading their education status. On the strength of this, visitors from abroad can still expect to hear from their Israeli guides that while there were no universities in the West Bank and Gaza Strip before 1967 'there are now six universities.' What this overlooks is that Birzeit has survived despite the occupying power's best efforts to destroy it, and the other universities have also been established without the participation of Israel.

The Israelis have not even provided real support, financial or otherwise, to any of these Palestinian institutions. On the contrary, the Palestinian universities have been supporting the military government. Over the years, Israel has taken taxes and customs duties worth many thousands of dollars from all of us. It is a practice which contravenes the international guidelines issued by UNESCO that advise member countries to exempt all educational institutions from taxes.

A typical example is the treatment of books. University books are not usually subject to taxes but we have to pay 15 per cent value-added tax (VAT) on all library and textbooks. Israeli universities are charged the same tax, but they are refunded annually. In any case, they are state universities, so this money merely represents a transfer of funds from one government department to another. Whenever we used to apply for the tax exemption (to which we were legally entitled under Israeli law) the answer we got was: 'We do not have the funds to pay you back.' According to the law, it was up to the military governor of the occupied territories to refund us the money, but he never did.

No less important, the new universities that emerged in our wake

Students at a sit-in strike in the old campus protesting against the move to the new campus, 1984

were quite different from Birzeit. What the Israelis can claim is to have helped to establish the Islamic College in Hebron. In 1971, Sheikh Mohammed Ali Ja'bari, the Mayor of Hebron, had started to talk about establishing a 'West Bank University' in collaboration with Israel, and eventually laid the cornerstone for a college there. However, it was a Shari'ah institution. The majority of Palestinians were against the establishment of the Shari'ah College, because this did not seem an obvious educational priority. Even the 'financial assistance' the Israelis provided to Hebron's Shari'ah College was minimal. They seconded a few teachers from government schools which were under Israeli administration to teach at the college and gave them just enough money to build a wall around its land. The college library resources were hardly sufficient for a high-school library. It was poorly staffed, and nobody wanted to go there apart from poorer people who did not have the money to go to a university abroad. However, when the college developed into Hebron University, the situation changed for the better, and the university severed its relations with the occupying authority.

Like everything Israel does to the Palestinians, the explanation for this odd burst of generosity lies in the way it served Israeli political ends. All that mattered to the Israelis when they had helped to set up Hebron College was that, they hoped, it would be anti-PLO. This was a disastrously short-sighted perspective and now, of course, Israel is reaping the reward for their policy of encouraging Islamist groups.

The new university in Bethlehem is a different story. Established with the support of the Vatican, it was built on existing resources. Its basis is the long-established Catholic high school, Frères College, run by the De La Salle order. The college upgraded itself to a university in the academic year 1973/74. It is lucky enough to be financially supported by its co-religionists abroad. However, even with all its international connections, the university was no safer than the other Palestinian universities when it came to Israeli punitive and oppressive measures.

Other Palestinian universities such as An-Najah in Nablus and Al-Quds in Jerusalem, although officially allowed to exist by Israel, also shared the same fate as the other universities regarding Israeli harassment. In defence of their negligence of the Palestinian educational system, Israeli politicians resort to a highly misleading use of statistics. They point out, for instance, that the number of students in the compulsory cycle in the West Bank went from 105,534 in the academic year 1968/69 to 143,918 in 1974/75, a growth rate of 36.4 per cent.

These figures, of course, constitute an improvement in absolute terms and the Israelis can claim credit for that. However, if you look at the 'control group', which is the East Bank of Jordan, you can see a different story. The number of students in the compulsory cycle during the same period grew from 283,006 to 472,309. This shows a growth rate of 66.9 per cent, which is almost double that of the West Bank.

Jordan is an excellent control group, as both the East and the West Banks were originally part of the same education system. If both started at the bottom of an imaginary scale and we now have a growth rate of 36 per cent, while Jordan has a growth rate of 67 per cent during the same period, this does not mean that we have improved by 36 per cent. On the contrary, it means we have fallen behind by 31 per cent. We should have done equally well, as we were part of the same system.

In 1967 there was only one government university in Jordan (the University of Jordan), but 20 years later the country had three major government universities, as well as at least six private ones. All the public universities in the East Bank were built by the Jordanian government, which provided them with the funds necessary to run and develop. All are of a high standard, with graduate programmes, medical schools, schools of engineering and other faculties.

During the same period, Israel did not establish a single university in the occupied Palestinian territories, while responsible for its governance. Instead they made it extremely difficult for all six non-governmental universities to operate.

The Israelis continue to try to take credit for the establishment of the universities in the West Bank and Gaza Strip, but the truth is that these grew in spite of Israeli impediments to their success, ranging from unfair taxation and the withholding of building permits to punitive closure. The outcome was a denial of Palestinian students' right to education.

Telling half-truths has, in fact, become standard Israeli policy. Another example of this is what happened when Israel occupied East Jerusalem in 1967. Teddy Kollek, the city's Israeli mayor at the time, proudly told the world: 'The first thing we did was to connect Jerusalem to a running water supply from Israel.' This could lead you to think that East Jerusalem had no running water supply then. Of course it did, but in order to 'unify' Jerusalem by separating it from the West Bank and collecting Palestinian taxes, the occupiers severed its West Bank water network and connected it to the Israeli network.

The Israelis could not make the same claims about East Jerusalem's electricity supply. The Jerusalem Electric Company, set up by Palestinians, supplied the city and the West Bank and it held a legal monopoly for both areas. As this meant the Israeli government could not legally supply the illegal settlements in the West Bank with electricity, the JEC also provided this service. Israel, though, did not like the idea of money going to a Palestinian company. Therefore, when the increase in demand inevitably created a need for larger generators, it banned the company from buying them. This meant that Palestinians had to buy their electricity from the Israelis, who presented their eagerness to supply it as an act of kindness.

I used to wonder why witnesses in court have to swear to tell, 'the truth, the whole truth and nothing but the truth,' but after hearing the Israelis utter half-truths for so many years, I understand that by withholding certain facts one can lie or distort things quite easily. This is what the Israelis have been doing for many years (see Appendix III and Appendix IV as examples of official Israeli claims and the Birzeit rebuttal respectively).

Certainly, when it comes to higher education, we do not owe the

Israelis anything. At best, Israel gave five other Palestinian universities permission to exist after we founded ours. However, none of them ever had the same inclusive, student body drawn from all parts of the occupied Palestinian territory that gave Birzeit its national character. Our students, too, continue to outshine those from elsewhere in academic terms. Keeping our academic standards high has been a principle we have upheld to this day against appalling odds.

What spurred our students towards success was the importance of a good education to a student's survival. Still, guiding them through a demanding degree course during a violent occupation was not easy. Some students had relatives in jail. Most had to run the gauntlet of Israeli soldiers patrolling our streets on a daily basis. Soldiers would amuse themselves by stopping young men carrying books, then order them to sing daft songs, insult their own mothers or stand on one leg in the rain for hours. A student who refused could expect a good kicking. If he fought back or even risked a defiant glance, he was sent to prison. Palestinians in the occupied territories can be held without charge or trial for 14 days.

How to keep up our students' spirits in the face of adversity? One boost was the start of building work on our brand-new hillside campus with its spacious lecture halls and labs. On inauguration day, students and staff shed tears of joy as we unveiled the large wooden 'Birzeit University' sign at the entrance. They then dried their eyes, quickly pulled out their cameras and started snapping pictures of themselves in front of it.

Reassured by the thought that Birzeit would soon be much less crowded, we could now also embark on a second uplifting project, an annual Palestinian Week in which we would celebrate our nation's achievements. Events included folk dancing, singing, poetry recitals and a display of landscape paintings. Regularly, at its opening, Professor Awartani would give a short concert of ancient tunes on his shepherd's pipes, a local instrument as old as the hills. After his arrest, fellow prisoners smuggled another one into his solitary cell, but the warders broke it.

During our national week, we flew the Palestinian flag and students were encouraged to bring in traditional costumes, jewellery and artefacts reflecting the richness and beauty of Palestine. We did not want the love of our country to be just an abstract thing.

Since Birzeit was educating students from a wide range of backgrounds I felt it was important to introduce an understanding of economics. Many parents had seen their livelihood destroyed by Israel in 1948 or 1967. Israeli imports were gradually killing off

Palestinian businesses in the West Bank. Fathers were unemployed and sometimes desperate enough to do construction work in Israeli settlements. Our students needed to know that their people had been good at farming, manufacturing and trade in the past and could be so again.

Until their expulsion in 1948, Palestinians had produced olive oil, rugs, pottery, glass, copperware, cigarettes, spices, clothes and the religious trinkets popular abroad, as well as the famous Jaffa oranges. These goods were all exported via Jaffa harbour. The city and harbour were over 6,000 years old; they pre-dated even the Hebrews.

To bring the Palestinian economy to life, however briefly, we decided to start something that was a mix between a harvest festival and a trade fair. Our students would obtain goods from local farmers and merchants, then display them for sale in various attractive ways. Tables were loaded with fashionable t-shirts, painted pottery, toys and processed food. There were carefully chosen samples of rattan furniture and carved olivewood. Huge baskets of pomegranates, citrus fruit, grapes and tomatoes would add colour and scent.

For some reason, this display aroused the particular ire of the military each year. As soon as it had been set up on the old campus grounds, soldiers would rush up to it and stamp on the displays or smash them with their rifle butts. At first, the students could only look on, angry and powerless, as what they had worked on for weeks was destroyed.

Gradually, though, some of our students grew more confident. Watching the display being prepared for one Palestine Day celebration, I saw the soldiers rush up, as usual, machine guns at the ready, and heard them shout: 'Go sit on your asses, all of you!' Instead of obeying, one young man, the organiser of the trade fair, walked up to the officer and said: 'How can you talk like that? You are insulting the ladies present; that's a bad thing to do.'

The officer looked astonished and the student pointed out that he had used a rude word. 'Most of us here come from the countryside', he went on, 'and we don't use words like that.'

Before the office could reply, the young man waved his hand at the tempting food display. 'You want yogurt?' he said. 'We can give you yogurt. You want ice cream? You can have ice cream. Take your pick!'

There was a long, rather disconcerting silence and I wondered whether I should intervene. Then, suddenly, the officer asked: 'Can you give me a cigarette?' Another student stepped forward and offered him one from his pack. The officer took it, murmured 'We are sorry,' and walked off with his men.

Sadly, this event did not result in a permanent change of attitude. Soldiers continued to storm the campus on a regular basis, shouting and breaking up whatever we had set up. Communications were difficult at best. Some officers had reasonable English and a few spoke good Arabic, but most knew only enough of our language to bark orders at us.

Anyway, student confidence was no substitute for an academic qualification. Having defined ourselves as a university was not enough. Birzeit needed international recognition, and this was the subject of much clandestine communication between Hanna Nasir and myself.

Given the ban which the West Bank's military governor had imposed on communication with Hanna, this required a variety of subterfuges. One method was to conduct three-way phone conversations via Switzerland; another, as time went by, was via Hanna's children, who were growing up in the States. I could receive calls in this way, although not actually make them.

Later, we moved on to a telex machine producing paper tape over a phone line, and eventually to a fax. I would send a message to a mailbox in the United States and then, at regular intervals, ring the number and start receiving whatever was in my mailbox. Fax machines were banned in the West Bank then, but we hid ours well.

The importance to us of such communication cannot be overstated. Birzeit was being suffocated; it was being strangled by Israeli measures taken not just against individuals, but also against the entire institution. Like intellectuals living in communist Europe at that time, we felt that to keep resisting the repressive Israeli regime we required a steady flow of information from outside and a strong, broad-based support network.

The military governor's attitude to this was threatening but vague. He knew that Hanna and I were likely to run into one another in places we both frequented, notably Amman and Beirut. Once I asked him: 'Suppose I saw Hanna on the street, what should I do?' He replied in a firm voice that I must immediately cross to the other side of the street.

So, for many years, Hanna and I discussed the university's education programme, problems and needs by indirect routes. Another major topic of discussion was our relationship with other Arab countries. The survival and development of the university depended on us maintaining good connections with the Arab world. Our funding came from various sources there, so information had to flow back and forth quickly and with as much detail as possible. Ordinary mail was not an option.

We also liaised with the PLO. This was punishable by imprisonment for anyone living under Israeli rule, if discovered by the military government. However, Palestinians had recognised the PLO as their sole representative since 1974. It was our government in exile, it acted as a welfare body for the refugees outside and it constituted the core structure of our future state. Outside Palestine, PLO members ran schools, hospitals and housing schemes. Most, if not all, Arab funding for projects in the occupied territories came through the organisation. Within the United Nations, the PLO enjoyed the respectable status of an observer.

Israel and the United States might consider the PLO a 'terrorist organisation,' but to us it was a liberation movement created by the Palestinians to represent themselves and keep their cause alive. It stood up for our people, whose country the Zionists had taken by force of arms and seemed determined to rid of its indigenous population. The PLO was determined to prevent the realisation of the Zionist dream of a purely Jewish state in all of historic Palestine.

In this spirit, we chose to receive our funding via an organisation called the Joint Jordanian–Palestinian Committee, de facto the PLO, though it was grudgingly accepted by the Israelis because of its Jordanian registration. They knew all about the way we were being funded, but seemed to prefer this to paying for Palestinian higher education themselves.

Still, being caught communicating with PLO officials directly carried a risk, so Hanna and I did not use anyone's real names even when talking on the telephone. To add a further element of safety, we used nicknames for any individual or institution we wanted to discuss, and we did so in English.

When we wanted to refer to Abu Ammar, the nom de guerre of Yasser Arafat, we used to call him 'the mason' or 'the carpenter', because in Arabic 'Ammar' is the builder, and we always used the English words. We would never refer to him in Arabic. Abu Ammar's second-in-command, Abu Jihad, was referred to by us as 'the pharmacist'. Even without agreeing such codes beforehand, Hanna and I could usually understand one another.

We would be more cautious when actually mixing with PLO figures, who took a great interest in our project. Even when we met with them in Europe and were staying in the same hotel, we never talked in public. Some members of the PLO, we felt, were too care-less about being photographed, unwilling to believe that pictures taken at meetings or events could find their way to the Israeli secret service.

Gradually, I got used to moving back and forth between the realm of the Israeli military and the forbidden world of Arab educa-tion sponsors and the PLO. However, I do not have a natural gift for subterfuge and this was to cause me problems. The first of these occurred even before Hanna was expelled.

A few months before his deportation, I had been crossing from Amman back to the West Bank carrying some documents from the University of Jordan, syllabus material and suchlike. Somehow, a mimeographed sheet of paper containing a PLO summary of an Israeli radio report had found its way into one of my files. It looked no different from the rest but as the Israelis on the crossing slowly went through every single one of my papers, they discovered it.

The soldiers searching me knew, of course, that I was travelling with Hanna, so they called both of us over. 'What's this?' the Israeli officer in charge asked, implying that I was carrying something illegal. I decided to act dumb. 'Let me see,' I said. 'Perhaps it's something that was lying around in my hotel room and I picked it up by mistake.'

I then pretended to read the page carefully, finally announcing that it was just a report taken from Israel Radio. 'I cannot not find anything illegal in it,' I told my interrogators. Of course what was illegal was that the page came from the PLO, revealing that we had been in contact with it. Still, I totally denied any knowledge of it.

The Israeli soldiers now took Hanna and me into another room and made us stand on opposite sides of it with our faces to the wall and with our backs to each other, so that we could not commu-nicate even with our eyes. The situation was absurd, but also so funny that Hanna and I struggled to suppress our laughter. Here we were, two middle-aged men with respectable university posts, being punished like small children.

A few days later, the military governor called and ordered me to write a letter of apology saying that I had carried the sheet of paper unintentionally. Otherwise, he said, the Israelis would take action against me. Having no choice I complied, but tried to word the letter so it would not incriminate us. Like everything else, though, the story was put on my record, which enabled the Israelis later to point to my huge file.

Hanna made fun of the incident because I had failed to check my papers and let that sheet slip in among them. Soon after, on another visit to Amman, he was crossing back, when he was caught with a Fateh paper in his bag. I do not know how it had got in but there it was and he was grilled even more intensively than I had been. It was not funny any more.

In any case, coming back to the West Bank from abroad was never easy for me. No matter when I arrived, an intelligence officer whom I came to know as Abu Saksoukeh (which means goatee-wearer) would always be waiting for me on the Allenby Bridge. I would be delayed for hours, as he went through every scrap of paper and every object I had brought with me. I was always the last passenger to get on the homeward bus.

So keeping up our Arab contacts was risky, but Birzeit needed a steady flow of funds to survive and I had no choice.

Equally crucial was a steady flow of papers, journals and books, unimpeded by the Israeli censor. Publications from the Arab world would be sent to Cyprus with Hanna's help. From there, a friend would send them on, not to Birzeit but to an Israeli friend of the university in West Jerusalem, who would then deliver them to us. Visitors from abroad were also often kind enough to bring along a couple of books, though the academic works we required could be rather bulky.

We gradually established an informal liaison office in Amman, in which a contact would let us know when a book courier was on his (or her) way, but we still needed to find a way of inconspicuously tracking down those couriers after their arrival in Palestine. New publications were eagerly awaited and widely shared at Birzeit. They were our only means of keeping abreast of current developments in literature, history, science and the study of politics. We were a Middle East university and needed to know what people were reading in the Arab world.

In exchange, we supplied Hanna Nasir with photographs of our events, information about our learning projects and literature about the university in general, which made it easier for him to raise funds for Birzeit.

We now had funding and books, but we needed more if we were to achieve our aims: credibility. Birzeit University needed to be accepted by its peers. As the first batch of students approached their graduation, we became concerned that there was no external mechanism for approving their degrees.

It quickly became clear that the Jordanians were not going to provide this approval. We suspected this was because they felt Birzeit was competing with their own universities, as well as because we saw ourselves as part of an independent nation rather than as part of Jordan. This was not said openly, of course. Instead the official reason given was that such a step would not help the Palestinian people. So we decided to approach the Association of Arab Universities (AAU) as a Palestinian institution. The AAU annual meeting in 1976 was being held in Iraq, in the Kurdish city of Sulaymaniyyeh, and Hanna and I decided to attend it together. We had obtained the endorsement of the PLO, as we wanted to emphasise the national nature of the university.

I still remember how nervous Hanna was, as the fate of Birzeit depended on the decision of the Association. However, once we made our pitch, the AAU members voted smoothly and unanimously to admit us. We had expected resistance from at least some Arab universities, because it was the first time a Palestinian university operating under Israeli rule presented itself to them and they wanted nothing to do with that country. What in the end resolved the issue was our endorsement by the PLO.

As a result of the AAU vote, we became the first Palestinian university in the Association. This was not only an important psychological boost for us, but it solved a very practical problem – the accreditation of the university and its diplomas. As a member of the Association, our diplomas were automatically certified by the government of Jordan and our graduates could work anywhere in the Arab world. Moreover, from now on any Palestinian university applying for membership of the AAU was expected to bring the endorsement of the PLO's Education Department.

Our first graduation ceremony, held in the summer of 1976, was a joyful occasion. The students had brought their proud parents along and we had invited urban supporters and friends. Peasant farmers, some of them illiterate, chatted to doctors and lawyers. The Palestinian flag and that of the university with the olive tree as its emblem festooned the stage where the ceremony was to take place.

Our symbol had been carefully chosen. What distinguishes the olive tree is that it can flourish even under the harshest conditions. Also, picking its fruit is always a collective effort, as the harvest season is very short. The resulting product, olive oil, is extremely nutritious and a staple of the Palestinian diet. Many of our students had learned about this form of agriculture only when they had helped with the olive harvest as part of their graduation requirements. Olive groves often belonged to small farmers now working as day labourers in Israel, and we knew that they needed all the help they could get.

Hanna Nasir, sadly, could not be with us, but we had asked him to record a speech for the occasion. He did this in a BBC studio in London and the tape was smuggled into the country. The secret had been kept right up until the moment when I stood up and announced: 'Now the president of the university will address the graduates.'

After that, the staff formally congratulated the first batch of young Palestinian men and women ever to receive a bachelor's degree from a Palestinian university. It was a great and very moving moment in our lives.

We now felt more confident, even sensing that we had something to offer the rest of the world. To enable people from abroad to share our experience of study and work, Birzeit founded an international summer programme. We already had some links with European universities, but were keen not to be always on the receiving end. When we sent our young people to study in Durham or Amsterdam, we wanted to give something back to the students of those institutions.

The course we were best placed to offer was Arabic as a second language. Students attending it would also learn about life in the West Bank, gaining first-hand information about life under military occupation.

Fortunately, Birzeit's Department of Languages had academic staff qualified to teach the proposed course. We also had lecturers in sociology and political science who could introduce international students to relevant aspects of their fields. Soon, the students attending our course did not just come from the universities we had relationships with in Europe and the United States, but from all over the world.

Some had heard about us through personal channels, while others had been alerted to our existence through friendly bodies such as the World Council of Churches or the United Nations Association, or through the Red Cross.

In 1978, we had set up a small outfit in London, the Friends of Birzeit (FOBZU), which sought to coordinate support for the university with the help of Birzeit graduates living abroad. Its director, Elizabeth Monroe, was a highly energetic woman who often managed to send us two or three study groups a year. She also arranged tours by academic experts, during which they would lecture at the university for a week.

There were other branches of FOBZU, including one in

Michigan, where there were many Arab-Americans. As its members were well-off, they would use their annual meeting to raise about three or four thousand dollars a year for Birzeit. Run by Karim Ajlouni, a lawyer, and his wife Suhaila, FOBZU Michigan's efforts allowed us to buy equipment we might otherwise not have been able to afford. However, while FOBZU Michigan was mainly established as a financial support organisation for Birzeit, British FOBZU sought to make the country's public and politicians aware of the problems the university was facing under the Israeli occupation. Spreading the word about Israel's harsh sanctions against Palestinian higher education was an essential part of our resistance to the occupation.

From the start of our summer programme, we put the emphasis on people-based learning. As our new international students were keen to study Arabic in an Arabic-speaking environment, we made special arrangements to ensure they had regular contact with our Palestinian students, who were attending different courses.

We also arranged for our young visitors to live in the university dormitories with our students. Members of our Student Council set up extracurricular activities and weekend trips to interesting places in the occupied territories for them. Friendships were forged and mutual understanding improved. The programme's quality kept getting better and better. Eventually, we extended it to become a one-year course called 'Palestine and Arabic Studies' (PAS).

In addition, we started to run a joint work camp, in which international students served as community volunteers together with our undergraduates. Some taught English, but it was mostly physical work, improving the local people's environment and our learning facilities.

A side effect of these schemes was, of course, that the students who came ended up witnessing at close quarters the way the army treated us. They took photographs, wrote letters and told stories about what they had seen when they went home after a few weeks. A few were already politically aware and empathised with the Palestinian people. Rather than just trying to tell the world what was happening to us, we could now also rely on them to tell the truth and nothing but the truth without embellishment.

There was an increasing amount to tell, because the level of repression was rising. Life under occupation was littered with human rights violations which gave the students a reason to protest. The local people who were arrested, maltreated, dispossessed or killed by the Israelis were their own friends and relations.

In order to put a stop to the protests, Israeli soldiers had moved on from just invading the campus grounds to breaking into our students' dormitories. There they would smash up the furniture, destroy students' books and notes, trample food and hit out in all directions.

The confrontation would usually start out as an Israeli response to a non-violent Palestinian protest march around Birzeit village. Having demonstrated, the students would normally walk back into the campus after a couple of hours. However, if the soldiers responded by rushing into the campus firing teargas and M16 automatic rifles, the students would start throwing stones. If they were dispersed, they would then withdraw inside. They always made sure they had buckets of water and onions to counter the nauseating, eye-burning effect of the teargas.

On one occasion, though, a number of students were staying in the dormitories because of sickness and did not join the demonstration. Soldiers running after the demonstrators found their way to the dormitory, broke the main door and stormed in and started raining baton blows on the heads of the students found there. They then pushed everyone out into the yard, despite the fact that the students were bleeding from the assaults inflicted on them. Windows and mirrors were smashed, along with any study materials they found.

The result of this attack was that 13 students with head injuries were lined up on the side of the road with their hands tied behind them. Negotiating on behalf of the university, I tried to persuade Major Maurice to let some of the teachers take the injured students to hospital. He refused to let them go. 'They will not die,' he said dismissively.

It was the kind of incident that would shock anyone but, sadly, not a totally new experience for us. By coincidence, though, it had been observed not just by our international faculty but also by a journalist. While talking to Maurice, I got word from my office down in the Old Campus that an American journalist and syndicated columnist, James Wall, who had an appointment with me that morning (set two weeks earlier), had arrived. Instead of meeting him in my office, I walked up with him towards the men's dorms.

At first, the soldiers would not allow us to approach the hand-cuffed students. Their officer warned us that his men would shoot us if we tried. However, James Wall ignored this and kept going, with me following behind, until he reached Major Maurice.

The Israelis now realised that they were facing an American journalist. So, when the reporter started asking the colonel questions, he initially pretended that he did not speak any English. As I explained to the reporter that the army was not allowing the students to be taken to hospital, the colonel suddenly decided to change his line. Determined to seem nice, he now announced that he had called an ambulance to pick up the wounded, which was not true at all.

The presence of an American witness, though, improved our bargaining situation. Thanks to Wall, we were able in the end to take all the 13 injured to hospital. No ambulance ever came, but we used two cars belonging to our staff.

No sooner had the reporter left, than the military commander of the West Bank and his liaison officer, Colonel Amnon Cohen, arrived at the campus. Cohen was a professor of Islamic studies at the Hebrew University and spoke flawless Arabic. I took both men around and showed them the damage which the soldiers had wreaked in the dormitory. The military commander was visibly upset, not about the deed itself but about the fact that it had been observed by an American journalist.

Amnon Cohen later came to visit me in my office. He clearly relished the chance to display his language skills and joked about the fact that I had called on the army to investigate the *Aathaar Al-'Udwan* (the traces of the crime). His joke didn't sound funny to me. I pointed out to him the broken, blood-stained baton left behind by his soldiers. 'This', I told him, 'is what your soldiers did. I will preserve the crime weapon here.'

Faced with such crimes, many of the visiting students and international staff took a very strong stand against the occupation authorities. They distributed materials to their embassies or consulates, joined demonstrations or mailed out protest letters. Some were manhandled by the Israelis for getting involved. After seeing Palestinian students attacked in the dormitories, a group of young visitors went to the American Consulate in Jerusalem to demonstrate and some were hit and injured by Israeli security forces there. Among the demonstrators were Belgians, Americans and Italians. All were arrested and, although they were released again shortly afterwards, the experience confirmed their understanding of Israel's suppression of any Palestinian viewpoint.

Our growing links with foreign academics, which were hugely important to us because they were professionally inspiring, sometimes had similar results. One week Birzeit played host to an American mathematician, Dr John Kelly. A world expert in topology, Kelly had travelled to the university in order to give a series of seminars. He had been invited to do so by one of our professors, who was the President of the Palestinian Society for Mathematical Sciences and had met him at Berkeley.

It so happened that the army decided to storm the campus on the day of Dr Kelly's talk. Soldiers poured in, firing live ammunition as well as teargas. Kelly, a frail, elderly man, was badly affected by the teargas and developed breathing difficulties. I had to lead him gently away to a bench some distance from the choking mist. We then got a student to hand him a cut onion so he could inhale its scent. The onion remains our sole weapon against teargas.

We could never have staged such an effective incident for conveying the nature of Israel's activities against Birzeit. Kelly recovered in time, but he was deeply shocked and ended up writing an article for the *New Yorker* about the situation.

We knew that just coming to stay with us and experiencing the situation for themselves would teach people all they needed to know about Palestine. We did not have to run any propaganda campaigns. In this, as in other aspects of the Palestinian story, we do not have to invent 'facts', as Israel does. We just have to make sure that as many people as possible are exposed to the situation as it is. Visitors just had to look around and they would see what Palestinians were going through. Even if they did not write anything, such people could give valuable information to reporters in their own countries. Our new foreign friends, Americans, British, German or French, would be present when a demonstration took place and witness what Israelis were doing to Palestinians. Some also took photographs and all were of enormous help.

What foreigners learned about was not just the experience of Birzeit, of course, but that of Palestinians all over the occupied territories. Many became devoted to the Palestinian cause. Palestinians did not have a functioning public information office then and what we told visitors was factual, reliable and clear. The university's public relations office was staffed by people who were gifted communicators. I often say that people found out more about Palestinians and their problems through Birzeit University than through any 'official' source.

None of this endeared Birzeit to the Israeli government. Nor, of course, did the military particularly like our international staff. Israel was always trying to get rid of these people one way or another. Giving foreign academics only short-term work permits was one ruse. However, we were usually able to keep those people in the country by other means. When the Israelis stopped issuing work permits altogether, lecturers wishing to teach at Birzeit started coming into the country as tourists, then renewed their visas every three months. It was not the best way of operating, but we were determined to solve the problem while observing the law.

By 1979 we had a flourishing campus, a growing network of supporters and great plans for academic expansion. In short, the future looked bright. We had no idea of the disasters that were just around the corner.

6

'CELLS OF ILLEGAL EDUCATION'

Each year on 15 May, Palestinians commemorate the *Nakba*, the events of 1948 that led to the loss of their homeland. It is a day of mourning for us, a reminder of the mass expulsions and destruction of villages wrought by Zionist troops. Birzeit students, like other Palestinians, usually demonstrate on that occasion. This often leads to clashes with Israel's army of occupation.

In 1979, Israel's 'Independence Day', whose date moves each year due to Israel's lunar calendar, fell on 3 May. All day, settlers had been driving past the university in their cars, shouting, waving flags and celebrating Israel's 'independence' in a provocative manner. Some students reacted to this by throwing stones at them. In response, the armed settlers started shooting at the students.

The Israeli army rolled up to support the settlers and there was a confrontation. I was called to the Post Office in Birzeit, which the Israeli army had turned into an operations centre. Colonel Feldman, the same military governor who had deported Hanna Nasir, took me to task about the students' behaviour. I told him that if settlers really wanted to avoid such clashes, they should keep away from the students. It would be best, I suggested, if the army advised the settlers to avoid driving through Birzeit, especially on such an emotive day. Instead, Feldman's soldiers went off and made all the students stand outside in the yard for hours, some of them in handcuffs.

Those forced to stand in the sun included Michael, an international student and the son of an American couple who worked as librarians at the university, Anna and Wayne Derrick. Michael got into a fierce argument with the Israelis and told Colonel Feldman that he was a liar. I froze when I heard him say this. To my surprise – and relief – Feldman did not respond. The students were eventually allowed to leave and the day passed without further incident.

The next day, though, Michael was interrogated at army headquarters and soon after he was deported along with his twin brother Karl, not as outgoing as his brother, and their parents followed shortly afterwards to be with their sons. Following this incident, the army ordered the university closed for an 'indefinite period of time'.

This was grim news. It also came at a rather inconvenient moment. Over recent months, I had developed severe back pains. By June I was in agony and it turned out that I had two slipped discs in my lower back. I had to go to hospital for an operation. Five days later, I was home but still suffering quite badly. Spinal surgery takes ages to heal.

Unfortunately, this was not a time even to think about bed rest. Without a functioning university, what would become of our students? What of Palestinian society? Birzeit needed to assert its rights.

We protested against the closure with a massive letter campaign directed to the media in the United States and Europe. In addition, we called on our contacts in the United States to encourage at least some congressmen to try to put pressure on Israel, so it would

Press conference at the American Colony Hotel after closure of the university by the Israeli military authority, 1979

rescind the closure order. Almost two months after the closure, George Assousa, an Arab American, who had contacts with the State Department, asked me if I was prepared to meet with the Israeli Minister of Defence, Ezer Weizman. I could then ask him to solve the closure problem.

I agreed, and within a couple of days, Assousa made the arrangements for the meeting. The problem was that I needed to travel to Tel Aviv. I asked Dr Antone Tarazi, the neurosurgeon who had operated on me, for advice, and he told me to lie flat on my back in the car for the entire journey. An army car from the military governor's office in Ramallah escorted us the entire way.

Weizman was polite and was joined in his office by the military commander of the West Bank, Binyamin Ben Eliezer ('Fuad'). The minister, a slim man with an old-fashioned British pilot's moustache, seemed a jolly, chatty fellow. He had commanded the Israeli flying squad that had bombed Jordan's airport during my brother's 1967 aborted honeymoon.

Weizman skirted around the subject for a bit. Instead of mentioning the closure, he talked about Karim Khalaf, the mayor of Ramallah, and Bassam Shak'a, the mayor of Nablus, in a friendly way. The two men were proud Palestinians and their cars had been booby-trapped some time ago by Israeli settlers. Bassam had lost both legs in the attack and Karim part of his left foot. Weizman referred to the former as a 'hard nut to crack'.

There was, of course, a connection with Birzeit. The year before, Israel and Egypt had signed the Camp David accords. This had been a great disappointment to us, as the accords failed even to mention Palestinian national aspirations. By signing them, Israel had gained recognition from the largest Arab state without offering freedom to the Palestinians. The West Bank was rocked by public protests and Birzeit's students had invited the mayors to speak at the university about their political views.

I told Weizman frankly about our students' feelings and made it clear that they needed to resume their studies. The university was a centre for serious learning, I explained. In fact its quality of education was so important to us that we picked applicants purely on the basis of their academic performance.

After I had expanded on this for a while, Weizman turned to the commander who was sitting on his right, and said: 'Fuad, my boy, let's open the university.' One could see from the way the two men communicated that they were good friends. Apparently, Fuad had served for some time under Weizman's command.

The next day, I was asked to meet with Fuad. He started our conversation by laying down conditions for a re-opening of the university. If we really wanted him to revoke the closure order, we would have to promise that there would be no more violent student protests.

I pointed out that I could not possibly make any such promises on behalf of the students. As a university, our role was to do our best to keep the place in order and to run the education process in a proper fashion. Fuad clearly did not like hearing this and the prospect of returning to our classrooms started to recede again. However, I remained optimistic and sure enough two days later the university was allowed to open again.

When I was in Tel Aviv, I decided to visit a potential supporter, the President of Tel Aviv University, Chaim Ben-Shahar, who had asked to see me. He was said to be vaguely sympathetic to Birzeit and he asked how he could help the university. I mentioned that one of the problems we faced was getting journals from the Arab countries, including the PLO's *Shu'oon Filistiniyyah* on a regular basis. Israeli universities had no problem obtaining such material and I wondered whether he could help. After thinking about this for a moment, Ben-Shahar offered to explore the possibility of channelling some of the journals to our library. Unfortunately, this turned out to be an empty promise. I never heard from him again and nothing came of his offer.

Moreover, no head of any other Israeli university ever enquired about the difficulties we might be facing as a university under occupation, or showed any interest in visiting us. All remained aloof, even when Birzeit was closed down. There was no sympathy whatsoever for our plight. You might have thought our university was on a different planet from theirs, yet the Hebrew University was no more than 16 miles away; most others were within an hour's drive. It was as if, in the view of Israel's academic leaders, Palestinians' attempts at organising higher education were beneath contempt. Preoccupied with their own grim past, Israeli academics seemed indifferent to the sufferings of others.

Over time, we managed to build links with a handful of sympathisers, the 'Solidarity Committee with Birzeit University', which was active in the 1970s and 1980s. But it was three decades before a group of the country's higher education professionals issued its first joint protest in 2008 against the restriction of academic freedom in Palestine. Even then, no university rector signed.

Birzeit's closure lasted for a full two months in the end. It also

Israeli Solidarity Committee visiting Birzeit University, 1980

set a new precedent by depriving Palestinians of education for a significant length of time.

We realised that these orders were not just a new way of punishing our students for demanding their national rights. Used often enough, they would eventually turn us into an ignorant, disorganised, fragmented and easy-to-control subject population, or so the Israelis clearly hoped.

We could not allow this to happen, but the problems facing us were formidable. Students whose parents had scrimped and saved to send them to Birzeit and who had themselves worked hard to achieve their academic aims had suddenly been deprived of access to education. Fourth-year students needed to prepare for graduation and take their final exams. Many students could not afford to hang around and wait for the university to reopen. They needed to complete their studies and start earning their keep. With the possibility of a graduate job receding into the distance, some girls were encouraged by their families to marry instead.

Faced with those prospects, we racked our brains for ways to keep the education process going. We needed to find other places in which to teach and ways for the students to make up for lost time.

By the third Israeli closure, we had formulated a back-up plan. As soon as a closure order was issued, effectively turfing us out of the university, secretaries would grab their files and teachers their books. News would then be circulated about the locations in which secret classes would be held. Science students, whose practicals could not be shifted elsewhere, would be smuggled into the campus at night to do their lab work. A student who needed specific books would indirectly contact our librarian, who would climb into the closed library through a back window, find the volumes in question and pass them to the student outside.

None of us was ready to give up, but the challenges this form of alternative education would throw up for us proved far greater than expected.

The first of these derived from the fact that many of our students lived some distance from the Birzeit–Ramallah area. Closures were invariably accompanied by an increase in military checkpoints. Youngsters carrying book-bags could expect to be stopped, searched and sent back. Anyone objecting to this, or even casting a defiant look, risked a severe beating plus a couple of weeks in jail. Students took to staying over at friends' houses near the campus or found ingenious ways to bypass the checkpoints, which often involved a long trek across hills.

We held classes in private homes, fields, company offices, mosques and churches. The whole community pulled together to lend premises and support our continuing efforts to keep the university functioning. During weekends, junior schools would sometimes let us use their classrooms (the Roman Catholic school nearby was very cooperative). Students and lecturers would make their way cautiously to a location whispered to them, then try to get on with academic work. In return for this local help, the university provided services to the community. Our students started to teach in neighbourhoods whose schools had also been shut down. This was important, as the military governor did not allow any school, once closed, to extend its school year. He considered the year to be completed even if pupils had been taught for a mere 50 days of it. We also set up support groups for the unemployed and for families who had lost their breadwinner. Both staff and students would collect food and clothing and distribute it to needy families.

Meanwhile, soldiers would scour the town for such classes. What this often meant was that they would look inside buildings for young people with books sitting around a table. Having identified them as students engaged in the illegal act of furthering their education (to be gambling instead would presumably have been legal) the soldiers would storm in and try to arrest all those present. Our university's financial manager, Harbi Daraghmeh, who was an undergraduate during several periods of closure, still remembers how students tried to escape by jumping through windows or running across roofs.

The Israeli army would frequently announce: 'We have uncovered cells of illegal education. We believe there are more of them and will remain in pursuit.' The term 'cells of illegal education' was eagerly adopted by Israeli politicians, who seemed unaware just how absurd it was.

Nevertheless, both academic staff and students caught in the education raids were often sent to jail. Even Israel's statute books do not list a crime called 'running a cell of illegal education', and so military judges would convict them of public order offences instead.

To bypass the army, we also experimented with holding classes in Jerusalem. Having been annexed by Israel against international law, the city was not technically under military occupation, so West Bank rules did not apply there. Birzeit maintained friendly relations with St George's, a highly reputable Church of England school. Many of its pupils came on to study with us and so it agreed to help. Teaching space and facilities were put at our disposal. As we were still allowed to enter the city in those days, teaching at least some of our students on its premises seemed to offer a solution.

However, the army quickly found out about these arrangements and started to threaten the school. The headmaster was told that the Israeli authorities would take action against him if he helped university students to meet on his premises. This put us into a very difficult position: although it seemed unlikely that the Israelis would carry out their threat, we did not wish to bring harm to this excellent school.

While the headmaster was still considering his decision, Israeli soldiers (who were plentiful in the city despite its civilian status) swooped on a group of our students who had gathered outside the school. It was no longer a safe environment. This was an unhappy outcome, not just for us but also for the school. After some discussion among our staff, we decided to abandon the arrangement, cancelling the classes that we had arranged there.

Jerusalem's YWCA and YMCA, institutions, which have long offered facilities to Jerusalem's Arab community irrespective of religious affiliation, were also sympathetic but had little space to offer us. Still, we decided to teach some of our students there, those who were already living in the city. But we could send out lecturers in only a few subjects.

Israeli Solidarity Committee visiting Birzeit University, 1980

Continuing to study under such circumstances required tremendous commitment, even on a good day. We had to make do without phones, photocopiers or a cafeteria. Our first-year engineering students were taught calculus in a rented room in al-Bireh, physics in Birzeit's student hostel, and chemistry in Jerusalem. Each journey meant that the student had to cross at least one checkpoint and so carried an inherent risk of arrest.

Not only did this mean that students regularly missed classes, but their degree courses became discouragingly long. As detention periods increased, some first-years had to restart their courses two or three times.

Eventually, our Israeli lawyer, Lea Tsemel, raised the issue of closures for an 'indefinite period of time' in the High Court and we obtained a ruling saying that a closure should be for a 'reasonable' period of time. This ruling was observed, especially during the subsequent closures of 1981 and 1982 – but that period was never less than two months. During that academic year alone, we were closed three times, twice for two months and once for three months. This cut a total of seven months from one academic year.

The third closure of the university in 1982 was especially galling, as it was caused by the Israeli invasion of Lebanon. Having marched into a sovereign neighbouring country, carpet-bombed its capital and then helped its local allies to slaughter thousands of Palestinian refugees, Israel nevertheless insisted it was a highly vulnerable state.

As such, it could not allow strong, dangerous institutions such as Birzeit University to operate.

Over the years, the closures became an increasingly distressing feature of our lives. One of their main effects was to prolong the time a student needed to complete his or her degree. To understand how this worked, it helps to look at the experience of two individual students.

Tahsin Alyan from Jalazon was planning to study English literature, and he arrived at Birzeit when the university was shut. All we could offer him were informal lessons, which were frequently interrupted by army raids. Soldiers would throw teargas grenades into the room to force all the students out, then split up so one group could arrest those who fled while the other would destroy science equipment or photocopiers and, later on, computers.

Tahsin could not always attend even those unsafe classes, because he was often turned back at one of the checkpoints between his home in the refugee camp of Jalazon and the university. On one occasion a soldier manning the checkpoint arrested Tahsin because he refused to sing an Arabic pop song when ordered to. Another time, soldiers came to Tahsin's home at night, to take him to prison. Before delivering him up, one of them told him not to kid himself that he would be treated well because he was a student. 'Things are different here from how they are abroad,' the soldier explained.

They were indeed. Tahsin was held for two weeks in a tiny, box-like cell and not allowed to see anyone. Moreover, as he had been arrested during his exams, he missed out on the credits. In the end, it took him five years to complete his degree. He was 26 years old when he could finally set out to find a job, a crucial step as he has a large, disadvantaged family.

Emad Ghaiadah had to wait eight years before he could graduate in his field, political science. This was partly because the university was closed down so often and partly because he spent time in jail.

Students who were in their first year when a closure occurred were most deprived, sometimes having to restart their course two or three times. What we tried to ensure was that finalists, at least, were prepared for their exams during a closure and had somewhere they could sit them. This, of course, assumed that they were free to do so.

Not surprisingly (to us, at least) the closures did nothing to lower the tension or change the anti-occupation mood in the West Bank. Angry, frustrated young people with nothing to do, and nowhere to go to, will find ways of expressing their feelings. This prompted what the military would describe as security-threatening 'flag incidents'.

Whenever someone raised the Palestinian flag, which was often, the military would instantly intervene. To the soldiers, the black, red, white and green flag was like a red rag to a bull. The fact that it originated at the time of the Arab Revolt, when Arab forces helped the British expel the Turks from Palestine during the First World War, was of no interest to them. They saw it purely as a reminder that the Arabs of Palestine, the original inhabitants, refused to go away and leave the land to the Jews. The students knew this, and regarded it as a challenge to hoist it wherever and whenever they could. Raising the Palestinian flag was a symbolic action, a sign of our struggle against the occupation, and the students' way of asserting themselves as Palestinians. The flag fluttering in the air affirmed our presence.

So flags were quickly and illegally hoisted from roofs, treetops and electricity poles. At one time the students managed to attach one to the top of the minaret in Birzeit village, at another time they flew it from the bell tower of the local Catholic Church. The soldiers would rush to get it down, but often could not work out how. Reaching high places like these clearly required a long ladder and they could not imagine how on earth the students had managed to do so without one. Neither, frankly, could I.

'Flag incidents' that involved a minaret or a church would often bring down collective punishment on a town. Shops or schools might be shut for a time, or local people would be made to stand outside the building for several hours. Soldiers would also randomly pick up young men, and at gunpoint make them climb up to bring down the flag.

The university would not be blamed directly if a 'flag incident' happened outside campus. One day, though, during one of the short stretches in which the university was actually open, our students managed to attach a flag to the roof of the student cafeteria in the Old Campus. This resulted in an almost instant call from the military governor. He did not just complain about the incident, but ordered me to have it taken down immediately.

My reply was that the university was not a military garrison. I did not have the kind of authority enjoyed by the military governor and the students were not soldiers. Therefore, I explained, he needed to give me time. This did not go down well. The governor threatened to close down the university and send his soldiers in unless I obeyed.

We couldn't always avoid following military orders, but there seemed to be no need to rush. It was noon, and we left the flag to flutter in the breeze for a bit. The military governor called again after half an hour, then again every half hour after that. At around four in the afternoon, I gathered the students and suggested that we salute the flag, sing the Palestinian national anthem, *Biladi* ('Our country'), and lower it ourselves. The students duly lined up, we saluted the flag and then slowly lowered it.

Our response prevented a confrontation and the storming of the university by the army. However, it did not increase my popularity with the military governor. The next day, he rang me up and insisted that this kind of incident must never happen again. I could hardly guarantee this.

Indeed, one bright, sunny morning on my way to campus, I noticed a huge flag, at least two metres long, hanging between the second floor windows of our administration building. No one could possibly miss it. I went into my office, secretly thrilled at the sight, and decided not to do anything about it.

As expected, I soon got a call from the military governor. 'There is a flag', he barked. 'Oh?' I said. 'I am not sure what you are talking about.' He described where it was and ordered us to take it down immediately. You cannot, of course, just say 'no' to a man commanding several hundred armed soldiers, and so I replied that I would see about this. We took our time, as usual, then pulled down the flag. We dispensed with the ceremony this time. I really did not know who had put it up, or how and when. Still, it was nice to set eyes on it once in a while.

On another occasion, Birzeit was holding a book fair in the yard of the old campus. As I walked up to give the opening speech, I saw two students carrying a giant Palestinian flag. Once I had taken up my position on the improvised outdoor speaker's platform, they stretched out the forbidden item right behind me. The event was widely reported in the press. The next day the governor called, asking me questions about it and wanting to know whether I had really stood in front of the flag. I brushed this aside, telling him that he ought not to over-react to such normal student activities.

Most of the time, though, we were playing cat and mouse with the military, trying to keep our students' education going outside when they closed the university. During the first intifada (1987–92) the YMCA premises in Ramallah became one of our key locations, where we would display announcements about students' classes. Although we had built up a good messenger system, it was not very fast, and this was the quickest way of notifying students of changes in their schedules. We could not actually teach in the YMCA, but used it for administrative tasks and as a staff common room.

The army was always milling around outside and one day soldiers tried to break in. YMCA staff held them off at first, but then asked me to come in. I arrived together with Albert Aghazarian. Walking up to the Israeli officer at the door, we explained to the officer that there were no classes taking place in that building. He refused to believe us and sent in his men. There was no way of stopping them. Once inside the building, though, the soldiers had a surprise. There were indeed no classes. However, there were noticeboards displaying the names of students who were graduating on such and such a date, as well as instructions telling students about to receive their degrees where and when to meet. These announcements showed that we had an ongoing education programme.

The soldiers, although disappointed by their failure to catch anyone in the criminal act of learning or teaching, photographed all they found. I later went to the office of the military governor to protest about the raid. He couldn't have cared less. Raids like this were almost routine.

What was striking about Israel's persecution of Birzeit was the weakness of the Israeli arguments when it came to justifying it. When talking to the local military governor once, I asked him to spell out his reasons for closing us down. His reply was that having over a thousand people together in one place constituted a 'security problem'. I resisted the temptation to point out that most of the world does not see an university in those terms and asked him to elaborate instead. He refused. The magic word 'security' was all that was required to shut us down.

Still hoping to persuade him, I went on: 'Look at it this way – if all these one or two thousand people are gathered in one place, at least you know where they are. You can control them. Now, though, they have spread out to 30 or 49, maybe 100 different villages. And if you regard the students as agitators, keep in mind that they can now agitate in all of these places.'

We ended up repeating this conversation, almost unchanged, every few months and the governor never offered us a deal. We had hoped that he might list some conditions which, if met by us, would lead to the university being reopened, but the Israelis clearly just wanted Birzeit shut.

From time to time, I asked for a meeting with the governor's superior, the military commander of the entire West Bank, but this was hardly ever granted. 'Fuad', that is Brigadier Binyamin Ben Eliezer, did not wish to see me. In any case, no Israeli official I talked to ever claimed that there was actually a law against teaching or learning. While our educational activities during closures were clandestine by necessity, they were not actually illegal.

When the closures began to be reported abroad, the Israelis did not like this and so gradually eased the pressure on our so-called 'underground education activities'. These had never been a security matter, of course. Faced with growing public resistance to their rule, the army had merely sought to assert its control over the streets.

So we kept going and even expanded our activities. As the standard of high-school matriculations declined, we devised our own university entrance exams. When the First Gulf War broke out in 1991 and Israel imposed a 40-day curfew that made travel impossible, we revised our graduation procedures. Students were allowed to sit their finals in Bethlehem or Gaza, as well as Ramallah. Most of them had been unable to work with us beforehand through the entire year's syllabus, so we sent out teaching notes and set up regional offices in which students could consult academic staff from various departments, as in an open university.

Meanwhile, the periodic reopening of the university was played for all its worth by the Israeli political sector. I would be called to the Ministry of Defence in Tel Aviv with the chair of Birzeit's board of trustees, Dr Darwish Nazzal, and our Director of International Relations, Albert Aghazarian, where we would be met by the defence minister and his officials. They clearly expected us to be grateful and were surprised when Albert snapped at one such occasion: 'You treat universities like shops, but education is an ongoing process. We have academic papers, scholarships and international accords to deal with, yet all you do is open, close, open and close the place again!'

The pressure which such restrictions and procedures put on our academic staff is hard to imagine. Still we held out, admitting students whether the university was officially open or not.

Closure orders normally came from the military governor. When the orders continued beyond the first and the second year, even the military governor was apologetic when giving us the news. The source of the orders, we knew, was the then Defence Minister, Yitzhak Rabin. It was he who had launched the infamous Israeli 'iron fist' policy against the uprising and so we were not keen to meet with him and glad that the other Palestinian universities had adopted the same policy. We were also aware that Rabin's government was beginning to come under some outside pressure about the closures.

We eventually met Rabin once. All the universities had been asked (that is, ordered) by the military governor to send their presidents and heads of their boards of trustees to meet him at the military headquarters in Nablus. There, Rabin told us that he might open the universities if things quieted down. We replied that there had been no good reason for closing down the universities in the first place.

I felt Rabin had not grasped the unpopularity of the occupation among all sectors of the population and had no real intention of re-opening the universities. We never met him again.

Eventually, Bethlehem University was to be the first to be reopened, in 1991. As usual, the Israeli propaganda machine started to spin right away. Two weeks after Bethlehem's reopening, a delegation from Europe's Lutheran churches was visiting Jerusalem. As its members were concerned about the welfare of the Palestinians, they met with people on both sides, including the new Minister of Defence, Moshe Arens. During that meeting they were told that Palestinian schools and universities were open and that everything was normal.

That very evening, the Lutheran church in Jerusalem had arranged a reception for this delegation. I was there and when they congratulated me on the fact that the university was now open, I had to point out that this was totally untrue. Only one university out of the six had been allowed to open. The rest remained very much closed. 'But the Minister of Defence told us a different story,' they countered. I explained that it was untrue.

The next day I went to the military governor and told him: 'You'd better open the universities, otherwise you turn your defence minister into a liar.' While this argument did not work, the authorities gradually rescinded the closures, one every six months. Birzeit was eventually to reopen after almost five lost academic years (see Appendix V for press release).

We held a huge, especially festive, graduation ceremony for six different intakes, whom I described as the 'wave of steadfastness and challenge' in my speech. We recalled those who had given their lives for freedom with deep sadness and the hard-won academic achievements of the students present with great pride. For the first time, we also formally hoisted the Palestinian flag.

7

'SHAKING OFF' AND BEING SHAKEN

One of the features of our resistance to the occupation was the almost universal Palestinian support for it. However, it is important to realise the human cost of such support. As the army increased its swoops, our young students and schoolchildren tried to take on the mantle of resistance. Some thought of it as playing Tom and Jerry with the soldiers and emerged unharmed. One of my science students, I discovered, had already served six months in an adult jail at the age of 14. As he shared his cell with a group of university students, they had taken turns to tutor him so he could pass his matriculation. He got the third best results in the West Bank.

Others were traumatised. Lea Tsemel complained to the military authorities that two of her clients had been so young they could not see above the dais when called to the defendant's stand. They were 12 and 13 years old, two young boys desperate to go home, but the judge had jailed them.

On 18 November 1980, the pupils of the Friends' (Quaker) Girls School in Ramallah went on a silent march through the town to protest against the wounding of students by the Israeli army the day before. One of the demonstrators was my 14-year-old daughter Hania. The military were everywhere in town that day, on the roofs of houses and out in the street. Hania was advancing with a group of classmates on the town's main square when some soldiers opened fire. She fell to the ground, her leg covered in blood. Her friends wanted to help her but she told them to run for it.

As she was creeping slowly along a side street a soldier walked up to her, kicked her hard and ordered her to walk. Bleeding and crying with pain, the girl obeyed and hobbled toward the army's jeep (a scene which was captured by an ABC camera team and later screened on their *20/20* programme).

Perhaps the presence of foreign witnesses led another soldier to show mercy to Hania. He lifted her up and then helped her to get inside the jeep. After a while, she was driven to hospital. When my wife arrived, Hania was in a terrible state. She was sobbing with pain and fear, saying: 'Mummy, please, don't let them cut off my leg.'

A couple of days later a man from the military walked into the hospital where Hania was staying, still under police surveillance and asked to see Hania to interrogate her. Haifa shouted angrily at him 'You shoot them and then come to interrogate them?!' and did not allow him to see Hania.

However, the army was not so easily put off. When she left the hospital, still on crutches, two months later, Hania was summoned to the local police station. There, they not only finger-printed her, but interrogated her like a criminal. I was furious and called the military governor who apologised and said that he would close her file. Through actions like this, the military government reverses the roles so that the victim suddenly becomes the aggressor and goes on the defensive rather than going ahead and demanding his or her rights as a human being, including the ability to raise a case against the injustice. Four years later, when Hania wanted to go to the United States to continue her engi-neering studies, she wrote in the visa application form that she had no police record. The consulate informed her later that she actually had a record and that this incident had been recorded by the soldiers against her.

Hania's suffering, though, was by no means over. Her tibia had been shattered by an M16 automatic rifle, and although the bone was fixed, her wound took a long time to heal properly. She was stuck at home for months, a depressed and traumatised teenager, unsure whether she would ever walk again. Luckily, Hania could eventually walk normally and even run, although the ugly scars remain, and not only the physical ones. Several of her friends who were injured that day were not as fortunate and were left with permanent injuries such as a bad limp or a permanent disabil-ity. Though a very strong woman, Hania still cannot bear seeing soldiers or even violent films. That is one reason she rarely comes to visit Palestine.

I had been in a hotel in Geneva when Hania was shot. Haifa had phoned me after seeing our daughter, but as she did not want me to worry while I was away she insisted that our daughter was fine. On the strength of this, I went on to Tunis for the annual meeting of the Association of Arab Universities, but then decided to cancel a visit

Hania on crutches on our front porch, 1980

to a Middle East Council of Churches meeting in Cyprus. When I
arrived at the Allenby Bridge on my way home, the Israeli officer
there announced that I was under arrest. I was put in an open-top
jeep as if to parade me all the way from Jericho to the police station
in Ramallah.

At the police station, I was allowed to call the hospital to hear how my daughter was, but could not talk to her. I then asked Haifa to call my lawyer, Elias Khoury. I also wanted to speak to the military governor, but the officer at the police station would not get off the phone. I had no idea why I was under arrest. After all, I had been away when all the disturbances took place.

Eventually, Elias Khoury arrived and asked for me to be released on bail. This was accepted without much ado, which suggested that my arrest had been a mere charade, designed to harass me and make it less likely that I would complain about my daughter's treatment. Once released, I rushed to Jerusalem to see Hania in hospital. I was shocked to see the state she was in and felt bad about having been away.

That day, ten school students had suffered a similar fate to Hania's. Some were never able to walk again at all or were permanently disabled in other ways. The only unusual thing about Hania's case was that she came from a well-known family. Immediately after the incident, my wife had received phone calls from numerous foreign journalists we knew, asking: 'Is it true that the Israelis shot up your beautiful daughter?'

Haim Gouri, now an Israeli journalist, came to visit us. Afterwards, he wrote a piece about how the girl he felt he had helped bring into the world had been shot by another soldier. The article was compassionate and indicated the type of person Gouri was. As the number of children killed by machine-gun fire started to rise, even some of his colleagues were disgusted by the army's claim that its soldiers were merely firing into the air. One Israeli columnist wrote, in an ironic vein, that 'presumably Palestinian children fly through the air. How else, otherwise, could they have been shot?'

Our experiences dealing with the Israeli occupation and with the military's harassment showed that a firm, direct response could sometimes temper the effects of their oppressive measures. But occasionally the best way to keep the university alive was to play 'the paper-clip game'.

We decided to adopt this policy when faced with yet another new military order. In July 1980, we received a message from the military commander in the West Bank sent to all heads of universities, ordering us to meet him at his office where he handed us Military Order 854. The order constituted, 'simply' as he put it, a modification of the Jordanian Education Law No 16 of 1964 which stated that 'the Minister of Education is in charge of all educational institutions, except institutions of higher education.'

In the course of modifying the law, the military governor had removed the last part of this sentence. By leaving this out, he had put himself in charge of all institutions of higher education as well. This meant that now all educational institutions were under his command, including our universities. It enabled him to control their key activities, which included the hiring and firing of academic staff and the admission of new students.

Like so many of the activities of the Israeli government in the West Bank and Gaza, Military Order 854 constituted a clear violation of international law. Relations between the universities and the military government deteriorated even further when the governor demanded to see the names of all students applying to the university before they were admitted. The Council for Higher Education condemned this encroachment on Palestinian education and its violation of the academic freedom that the universities were supposed to enjoy. Naturally all Palestinian universities agreed to resist the order and its implementation.

Having been rebuffed, the governor sought a different channel through which he could impose his control. What he alighted on were the work permits that his office issued to international academic staff. At that time 25 per cent of our faculty members were in this category. Some were Palestinians with foreign passports (who counted as non-residents), while others were foreign nationals.

The governor now decreed that every foreign member of our university's academic staff needed to sign a statement, which later came to be known as the 'loyalty oath'. Lecturers wishing to be issued a work permit had to state that they abided by Israeli rules and regulations. One of these regulations, number 18, stipulated that such people were not allowed to have any contact with the PLO or any other 'terrorist' organisation. Nor could they refer to such organisations in complimentary terms. The military governor's office started to send out this statement with every application form.

This created a dilemma for academic staff who refused to equate the PLO with terrorism. Those whose temporary visas were about to expire came under pressure to sign, despite their reservations. France was the only government to back its nationals when they refused to sign, and so their visas were renewed. Britain and the United States did not want to get involved, and this meant that their nationals faced the stark choice of either signing or being deported once their visas expired.

As a result, anxiety and unrest spread in the university. Students went on protest strike and numerous articles attacking the 'loyalty oath' appeared in the papers. The best was written by five academics from the Hebrew University.

At the time, the assistant military commander of the West Bank was Colonel Yigal Karmon, later to be anti-terror advisor to the Israeli government. When I had a meeting with him over this business, I insisted that there was no way he could enforce this order. 'If you do not want to look bad and since you cannot implement it,' I said 'why not just freeze the process and finish with 854?'

I also reminded Karmon that a group of academics from the Hebrew university had written an excellent article about the illegality of 854 and had described it as totally useless. He dismissed this by saying, with a wave of his hand, that the authors of this piece were 'communists'. I pointed out to him that actually one of them was a religious Jew. Karmon did not know how to respond, but the issue remained unresolved for the moment. (See Appendix VI for the Report.)

Wondering how to deal with this dilemma, I looked at the list of items on the form sent to our foreign faculty members, and came up with a ruse. I told our personnel officer Assem to remove item no 18 from the list and photocopy the sheet again. This seemed the only way to save those of our colleagues who currently held temporary visas but needed residence permits. If they left now, we feared, they would not be allowed back.

It took some time to prepare and distribute the edited forms to the staff and to get them signed. I then sent them off to the district officer, Captain Roni, who declared himself delighted. Birzeit, he concluded, had finally submitted to his authority. He must have been so thrilled that he failed to scrutinise the form. Three days later, alas, the Israelis noticed the missing item.

I was called, interrogated about the change in the document and accused of forgery. My lawyer, Elias Khoury, argued that it was not really an official document but a mimeographed sheet which you could fill in however you liked. The Israelis had to accept this as we were right in legal terms (see Appendix VIIa and VIIb, work permit forms, in which item 18 was removed from the latter).

Sadly, however, the Israelis failed to concede the point of principle behind our lecturers' refusal to sign. This was that Birzeit was an autonomous Palestinian academic institution and had the right to choose its own staff. Soon after, the Israelis' anti-Birzeit campaign was stepped up a notch.

The authorities appointed an education officer for the West Bank, a man called Gabai. I was told to meet him at the new education office, which was situated in the army headquarters in Beit El, where the Israelis also built a settlement with the same name. Gabai tried to be friendly and explained that he was keen to cooperate with us. I replied that he could help by staying away from the university, and if he wanted to help even more, by freezing Military Order 854.

Naturally, my answer did not go down well. The officer then contacted me to say that he wanted to pay me a visit at Birzeit. I replied that he could tell me whatever he wished by phone, but was not welcome in the university. Nonetheless, he rang me a few days later to say that he would drop by. He was trying to show us that Military Order 854 was in force and that he was in charge.

As soon as I heard this, I went to the office of Dr Izzat Ghourani, our Vice President for Administrative Affairs, as I did not want to meet Gabai in my own office. The education officer arrived alone and, it seemed, did not walk in through the university's main gate but through a side entrance. As a result, nobody warned us of his coming.

I had hardly started talking to him when I heard raised student voices and other noise. The students thought Gabai was a settler because he was wearing civilian clothes and a skullcap, and they were both afraid of him and worried for me. Gradually, the yard outside filled with angry young men. The Student Council insisted that the officer had to leave. I told Gabai he had put us and himself in a difficult position.

I then went outside and told the students: 'Listen, the man is already here. We have to get him out but you must be careful. If anything should happen to him, it will be an absolute disaster for us all.'

I then announced that I would leave the building together with Gabai and asked Sami 'Ayed, a member of the Student Council to accompany us. Gabai, I noticed, was getting very nervous. He could not possibly imagine just how nervous I was feeling. As we walked from the office towards the stairs, Sami followed behind. A mass of students were thronging the staircase. One of them pushed Gabai and he came tumbling down the stairs.

I was in front, so I stumbled as well. The students had closed the gate leading from the yard to the street and, once I was upright again, I told them to quickly open it. Gabai got up again and walked out into the street. He then pulled out a revolver, fired some bullets and screamed into his walkie-talkie for help. When he had been pushed, his glasses had fallen down and the students retrieved them and later gave them to me. Two hours later, I took them back to Gabai at the post office in Birzeit and made sure that he was all right.

What had also fallen off at that tense moment was Gabai's skull-cap, and the students set fire to it, furious at his imposed visit and at his firing of the gun.

The authorities subsequently accused us of having made an anti-Semitic gesture and the incident resulted in the closure of Birzeit University for the second time that year. The event was hugely exaggerated by the Israeli media so as to justify the closure. In response, I argued that the officer had come uninvited and without giving us proper notice, sneaking into the university through a side gate. Ours was an independent university, neither founded nor funded by Israel, and he was representing military control. The students had been hostile, but they were afraid that he might harm Birzeit.

It is important to understand here that after so many years of occupation our young people don't know Israeli Jews as anything but oppressors, people whose entire lives seem geared towards making ours impossible. 'The Jews are coming' to young Palestinians presages the dragging away of a protester, the raid on an institution, the shooting of children. The arrival of even a single Israeli official may herald the uprooting of a farmer's trees or the demolition of his home.

Our students understand that an Israeli wearing a skullcap is an orthodox Jew. However, the only orthodox Jews they've ever met are settlers, people whose desire to take our land and expel us is virulently explicit and occasionally embarrasses even the more secular military men.

The younger Palestinians have never had the kind of experience of Jews that I had when I was a child in 1930s Jerusalem. My father's architectural assistant was a man called David Ginsburg. He would have long conversations with my father, saying that he felt more in common with people like him than with the orthodox Jews living nearby. Our two families were friendly and visited one another. Parents and children would sit in the lounge and drink sweet tea, which was accompanied by each community's type of sweets. We also exchanged presents at Christmas and Hannukah.

In 1967, Ginsburg and his wife came to visit our family in Ramallah to check we were all right. Their son, though, was now a soldier, part of an army which was holding absolute power over us. My children have only known Jews as soldiers or settlers.

A few weeks after the education officer's visit, Sami 'Ayed was blamed for Gabai's fall and given a prison sentence. Fortunately, the case against him was later dropped for lack of evidence. The fact that Gabai's eyeglasses were intact when we returned them to him after the incident helped expose the lies about the seriousness of his fall. The visit had almost ended in disaster and I remembered it for a very long time. Still, it discouraged Israeli officials from turning up at the university on a whim to assert their alleged authority over us. So the incident did not have an entirely bad outcome, after all.

While we sometimes managed to restrain students from actions with potentially dangerous consequences, we could not isolate them from major events in Palestine, even if we had wished to. The upsurge in land expropriations, the growth of Israeli settlements and the increasing use of machine guns against unarmed protesters fuelled Palestinian anger.

In 1984, the first Palestinian student was shot dead by soldiers on the Birzeit campus. The victim, Sharaf At-Tibi, was in the fourth year of his engineering course. A popular young man but not very political, he had been an active member of the university's folk dancing troupe. Another student, Mohammad Dhahab, was killed in 1986. Rather than apologise, the military government had responded by closing down the university again.

In 1987, the anti-occupation protests which had been growing in the West Bank exploded into a mass uprising. The trigger was an incident on 8 December 1987 in which an Israeli military vehicle ploughed into a group of Palestinian workers from Gaza. Four of them were killed and three more badly injured.

These were not the first deaths among this disadvantaged and much exploited group. Some time earlier, a 16-year-old Palestinian boy working for an Israeli farmer had been beaten to death by his employer. Palestinian labourers sleeping in an old air raid shelter near their job in central Israel had died from smoke inhalation when they tried to light a fire inside to keep warm, and could not escape as they were locked in. The truck incident, though, was the match that lit the fire of revolt.

This intifada (which means 'shaking off' in Arabic) was a popular mobilisation that drew on the informal organisations and institutions that had developed under occupation. It rapidly acquired the support of hundreds of thousands of people, many with no previous resistance experience, including children, teenagers and women. Local people embarked on varying forms of civil disobedience, including massive demonstrations, the building of barricades, general strikes, refusal to pay taxes, boycotts of Israeli products and political graffiti. There was also an intensification of 'illegal' education.

A clandestine leadership soon emerged and started giving daily instructions to the population. Business strikes were held on certain hours of the day, to which the army reacted by decreeing that all shops had to be opened regularly. Soldiers would go around breaking the locks of shops, so as to force shopkeepers to stay inside and guard against looting. However, solidarity among the population was so great that no looting ever occurred and shopkeepers stuck to the instructions of the intifada leadership.

To break the strikes, the army would resort to threatening the shopkeepers with being shut down permanently or tried to blackmail them with any information it had. Those who refused its demands were dragged to the local military headquarters (the Muqata'a) and kept there for hours, but this kind of persuasion also did not work.

Students reacted by throwing stones at the soldiers, burning tyres and demonstrating in all sorts of places. Sometimes children were the ones leading the struggle. The situation led quickly to the army starting to close the schools and universities as a pre-emptive measure. As the university was closed for ever-longer periods, we started to joke that the Israeli government was trying to save on paper. Students were continually attacked by the army. Anybody caught with textbooks would immediately be targeted. This was the beginning of Birzeit's longest closure.

With the intifada, the whole population revolted in an act of solidarity. The atmosphere became very exciting. The students' commitment to changing the situation was heroic at times, but both activists and others paid a high price. Some of this was due to Israeli misconceptions. The occupation authorities seemed not to understand that all our students would naturally see life under occupation as humiliating and unbearable, and so a search began for hidden leaders, shadowy figures seen as planting such ideas and corrupting their minds.

How does an occupying power identify leaders? Well, Israel had no compunction about using torture on a huge scale. Palestinians under interrogation have been clubbed, hung by their arms for days, immersed in sewage, burnt and given repeated electric shocks to all parts of the body, including the genitals. Ever more brutal methods were devised to extract names from the young detainees.

And, once alleged student leaders had been identified, they would be tortured in turn to find out when they planned to demonstrate again or to stone Israeli soldiers. The notion that many of these activities were spontaneous did not enter the interrogators' minds. Nor could they understand that in a situation like ours new leaders emerged constantly and were easily replaced by others feeling equally oppressed.

Students were stopped in the street and often beaten so badly that when they were taken into detention they arrived with broken bones or internal injuries. One early such incident involved a Birzeit economics student, Muhammad Shtayyeh, who had been detained on 1 January 1977 by a group of soldiers because he was carrying university textbooks. He was beaten until he lost consciousness before being thrown into the street. He required prolonged hospitalisation and his injuries were so severe that reporters from Associated Press and Agence France Presse came to see him in hospital, as did the US Consul General. The matter was even raised in the US Congress.

Soon after, Shtayyeh, an active member of the Student Council, was rearrested in his parent's home, handcuffed, blindfolded, put on a jeep and beaten all the way to the military headquarters in Nablus without being able to see who was hitting him. He was then sprayed with a strange-smelling liquid, made to wear orange overalls and put into a room full of ropes. These were used to lift him up so he could be handcuffed to a water pipe high up in the wall, with his toes barely touching the ground. It is a position that will cause a detainee the maximum amount of pain. First, the tight plastic handcuffs increasingly cut into his wrists. Then, as he gets tired, his body sags downwards, his arm muscles are stretched to breaking point and his shoulders are pulled out of joint. It is a torture method pioneered by the Spanish Inquisition.

Shtayyeh would be left in this position for days at a time. As he told us later: 'If you were hung from that water pipe on Friday, you would be there until Sunday, because the interrogators would go home for the weekend. There were no toilet breaks.'

Most of the time, his head was covered with a stinking burlap sack into which previous prisoners had vomited and he would vomit too. In addition, he was daily beaten all over his body. After 55 days of this, he was allowed to shower for the first time because the Red Cross had asked to see him. When given a mirror, he struggled to recognise his face. Moreover, his ordeal was far from over: he would serve 116 days altogether, with 65 of them in solitary confinement, and was permanently disabled. The cartilage of his knee had to be amputated because it had been damaged beyond repair by his torture.

Shtayyeh's experience was far from unique. Other students of ours have described some of the same torture methods to their lawyers. However, none of this succeeded in deterring them. Shtayyeh went back to his studies, remained active and eventually obtained a PhD.

In 1990 he returned to us from Britain as a lecturer, became dean of students, and in 1991 was the first Palestinian to land in Madrid for the peace talks with Israel. Since then, he has held several senior posts and is now the Director General of the Palestinian Economic Council for Development and Reconstruction (PECDAR).

The students' determination to resist also led the army to believe that West Bank teachers, lecturers and administrators were fuelling the uprising. The army's attitude to us and our families became increasingly hostile and the military governor took to sending for me any time of day or night, whenever he wanted me to open up the locked campus gate. His soldiers would march into our house without even knocking. Their manner of arrival would frighten the children, and one day Haifa got so distressed by their arrival that she snapped at them to go away. In response, a soldier hit her in the face. On another occasion, soldiers ordered our children who were still quite small to clear away a large pile of stones someone had piled up near our house. Haifa defended the children, whom the soldiers were trying to push outside, like a lioness.

Other Palestinian educationalists were also victimised. The situation was especially grave in Hebron, where young men from an illegal Jewish Orthodox settlement inside the town beat up the headmaster of the high school and several of his teachers after a pupil protest.

Following an incident in the same town during which stones had been thrown at a settler bus, armed settlers with their guns blazing broke into the Tariq Ben Ziyad high school. When the headmaster tried to block their way, the settlers kidnapped him. Taken to their settlement, he was threatened, manhandled and eventually handed over the Israeli army at another settlement, Kiryat Arba, and was interrogated for several hours.

Primary school children, too young to protest, sometimes suffered an even worse fate. In Nablus an eleven-year-old girl was shot dead and her nine-year-old sister severely wounded when shots were fired at them from a passing Israeli car during a pupil protest. The car had been driven by a uniformed soldier who opened fire after teenagers threw stones. The older sister had been shot in the chest at close range, the younger in the face.

Neither the very young nor the very old were safe. Soldiers took to lobbing teargas grenades into people's homes if there was a nearby pupil protest. The outcome was terrible. The highly toxic gas, explicitly marked as suitable for outdoor use only, paralysed the airways of babies and at least half a dozen of them died.

A witness report handed to a liberal Israeli parliamentarian called Seva Weiss revealed that after a stone-throwing incident in one West Bank town, the army devised an arbitrary kind of revenge. The report described how, in order to clear the streets of stones and refuse, including some heavy rocks, 'old men and women, arbitrarily chosen since the young men had all run away, were forced out of their homes, threatened with clubs, cursed and made to clean up the mess.'

In another town, some 50 people were arrested after an Israeli car had been stoned in an alley. They were lined up against a wall, then made to lie on their bellies and do push-ups. Anyone slowing down was beaten on the back or the testicles.

Palestinians taken to the Israel detention camp of Fara'a near Nablus, which held mainly boys of high-school age detained before trial, suffered a particularly harsh and humiliating regime. Three hundred of them were herded together in buildings which had served as stables for the horses of the British army before 1948. Large plastic dustbins were given to the prisoners for their sanitary needs and their hair was shaved off.

Of no security value, all those measures were an obvious attempt to destroy our dignity and create mental distress. Eventually, my turn came to experience this policy, literally in the flesh. One day, in between the various university closures, a group of soldiers tried to march into the campus. Worried that this might trigger a protest, I tried to block their way by closing the campus gate in front of them. After forcing it open, one of them then struck me on the head. I went down like a stone and could not get up for a couple of minutes.

The worst thing was not the injury. Although blood was running down the side of my face, I was not very seriously hurt. What was terrible was seeing the faces of the students and young lecturers who had witnessed everything. Some were transfixed with horror, others had tears in their eyes. A few were actually sobbing.

I did not at first understand the strength of their response. A few nights later, when a delegation dropped by our home to check how I was, I asked them to explain it. 'We felt as if our whole world was falling apart,' one female student burst out. Others nodded or affirmed what she had said, until things began to make sense: as the president of their university (nick-named 'the boss' behind my back) I was a figure of authority, someone they looked up to and could rely on in a world full of humiliation and brutality. Many had witnessed brothers or fathers being beaten in front of them. The university, however turbulent at times, was often the safest place they knew.

The shock and paralysis had not lasted long that day. As natural instincts kicked in, those who had witnessed the incident from the windows above started to pelt the soldiers with everything at hand, books, crockery and pails of dirty water. It ended up as yet another day of 'rioting' as the Israelis defined it, but some of the trauma stayed with those who had been present.

8

NOT OBEYING ORDERS

In the face of brutal Israeli attacks, and determined to avoid a similarly violent response, we were able to resort to civil disobedience as
a less traumatic way of asserting our independence and expressing
political views. As one section after another of Palestinian society
stopped obeying Israeli orders, at Birzeit we hit on a new way of
doing so ourselves. Since the university was closed by military order
during the first intifada and we were not allowed to operate, we
decided not to pay income tax, and suggested that all Palestinian
universities follow suit. In this spirit, we stopped completing the
monthly revenue forms on behalf of the employees and ignored the
repeated threats from the military government's tax department.
After a year or so, the Israelis started putting pressure on us. Since
we were already closed, they could not target the university, so they
instead picked on individual teachers.

The only hold the tax authorities had over our teachers was
linked to travel permits. Any Palestinian wanting to travel outside
the country required such a permit. Previously, this had been obtain-
able from local service offices on the way to the Allenby Bridge.
Now the governor issued a military order requiring people wishing
to leave the country to obtain a statement from the income tax
department showing that they had paid their taxes.

Academic staff could not obtain such a statement directly,
because their university was supposed to be deducting the tax from
their salaries. However, many needed to travel and gradually, pressure mounted from them to provide these papers. Since the universities were refusing to pay taxes to the military administration, they
could not do so.

There was a tug of war between the universities and the military
administration. We managed to hold our ground, since those who
wanted to leave approved of this act of civil disobedience by the
university. This state of affairs continued until the military government made a breakthrough. Its officers were able to get hold of the

During the graduation ceremony at BZU, 1992

budget of An-Najah University by raiding a bank in Nablus. One of its board members had a copy of the university budget in his office, which revealed the salaries that the university paid its staff. The military government confronted the university with this document, and calculated the amount that the university owed in tax on behalf of the teachers.

The military then added an exorbitant amount as a fine for late payment (quite illegal but this was used as a bargaining chip). Unless An-Najah paid, said the authorities, they would confiscate

After the graduation ceremony at BZU, 1992

university property such as study equipment and furniture and sell it at auction. An-Najah had to succumb and that forced all the other universities to follow suit. An individual university had only so much bargaining power.

Still, Birzeit had a good West Jerusalem lawyer, and he was able to negotiate a deal by which we paid as little as possible. The military government had to settle for this. It was a rather modest victory.

However much power Israel wielded through its military might in the occupied territories, we found ways to assert our independence and keep in our hands the control of our own affairs. One way we did this was by creating what was de facto a Palestinian Ministry of Higher Education in disguise. We did this by formally coordinating the activities of Palestinian universities. While my experiences were mainly with the running of Birzeit, universities in other parts of the West Bank and Gaza were suffering in similar ways from the harassment of their students and faculty by the Israeli military occupation.

The project to coordinate our activities was the brainchild of Mr Ibrahim Dakkak, the head of the Engineers Union and a member of Birzeit's board of trustees. It was launched at a meeting to which the elected mayors of cities and towns, the heads of all the professional unions (lawyers, engineers, medical doctors, pharmacists, dentists and veterinarians), the chairmen of the boards of trustees of the universities, the presidents of universities and colleges and several national figures from the community were invited. We excluded only colleges operating under the Israeli occupation authorities.

The meeting, in the spring of 1977, decided to establish a body that would supervise and coordinate all higher education activities. The problem was to avoid registering this with the Israeli authorities – who would, in any case, refuse to accept it – yet endow it with some legal status. Such a status was essential so it could operate in the occupied territories and the outside world, and so the Association of Professional Unions took this body under its umbrella. The first Palestinian Council for Higher Education (CHE) had been born.

The CHE had a general assembly made up of a broad national base and an elected executive committee. I was elected as Chairman of the Executive Committee and Mahdi Abdul Hadi, who was the public relations director at Birzeit, was secretary. There were seven other members, including the president of An-Najah University, the vice president of Bethlehem University and the elected mayors of Ramallah and El Bireh. Creating such a body was a major achievement for Palestinians under occupation, and a step in the direction of building the infrastructure for the higher education sector in Palestine.

To ensure that the Council would be of a Palestinian national character, we sought the approval of the PLO. Its Amman representative provided this. Thus the Council became the official representative of our higher education institutions and all funding was channelled through it. In the absence of a national government, the

Council for Higher Education (CHE) was the closest we could get
to a ministry of higher education.

In fact, the universities themselves were already doing much of
what is normally the job of a national government. At Birzeit we
had a centre for combating illiteracy which supervised and trained
teachers working in illiteracy centres all over the occupied territories. We also had a Centre for Environmental Health which worked
with our pharmaceutical companies to ensure the quality and
safety of the drugs on the market. Our Community Health Centre
promoted and developed primary health care in cooperation with
non-governmental health committees.

Yet another service CHE offered in the absence of a national
government was the provision of tertiary education of an adequate
standard (in our case I can say of a high standard) to Palestinian
students at 25 per cent of the normal cost. CHE ran a generous
financial assistance scheme for disadvantaged students.

Maintaining a high-quality educational system and providing this
service to all qualified students required funding beyond the capacity
of the universities themselves. They were able to raise funds, mostly
from Arab sources, for development but not for running costs. Even
Arab countries which had pledged to support the Palestinians under
occupation did not always fulfil their obligations. To ensure that
the payments were made, university heads sometimes had to travel
in order to lean on the funders. Nonetheless, the running budget
of the Council to cover the deficits of the universities grew as the
universities expanded, and by 1986 it was close to $15 million.

CHE helped solve much of the funding problem by organising
fair criteria for the distribution of funds based on categories of
expenditure, such as teaching staff, and facilities such as libraries,
laboratories and dormitories. It also devised systems of quality
assurance and regulated the launching of new programmes and new
institutions. What made its decisions acceptable was its local base,
as well as its PLO link. Over the years, the Council established itself
as the principal point of contact for higher education in Palestine,
and European and American governmental and non-governmental
bodies came to recognise us as such.

One of Israel's aims in dealing with the Palestinians is to conceal
or deny the existence of any cultural or social identity that is specifically Palestinian. It's easy to see why. If the Palestinians are seen to
have a history stretching back for hundreds of years, a rich culture
of literary and artistic expression, and a multi-layered society of
urban and rural communities, it weakens the case for the twentieth-

century influx of hundreds of thousands of European Jews into a 'land without people'.

Expressing our national identity was one of the ways in which Palestine's educational institutions could maintain awareness of our case against Israel, through projects initiated by student councils and paid for out of university funds. One such project was a large exhibition of books, art and sculpture produced by students who were political prisoners. These were displayed alongside original handicrafts and Palestinian manufactured products.

This annual event, which lasted for two days, ended with what was known as a 'Palestinian Wedding', in which students acted out all the steps of a traditional Palestinian marriage ceremony, including dances and songs. To make it more realistic, they sometimes even brought along camels and horses. This attracted not only the students and their families but also people from the community.

Unsurprisingly, the military was not keen on this event. While we were setting it up, Colonel Karmon, the deputy commander of the West Bank, came by one day and asked to look around. I carefully steered him towards some general display, but he insisted that he wanted to see the artefacts made by Palestinian political prisoners. However, by the time we arrived at that display, the students had been alerted and the officer looked slightly foolish inspecting a few tiny, innocuous items.

In the end, I explained to the colonel these items had been made

The author with the Pugwash Council, 1992

The author chatting with president of Pugwash Dorothy Hodgkin during the annual conference in Venice in 1982

by students who had been imprisoned for no reason. They had been detained illegally and I felt that we had nothing to hide. We were not doing anything wrong. In any case, I knew that some collaborator or other would eventually tell the military government about the exhibition. We were not engaged in some clandestine project. In our university, we believed in freedom of expression and students were allowed to express their national feelings.

On another occasion we held a big book fair. The army's response was to close the university and confiscate some of the books. The authorities then justified the closure by arguing that there were books inciting against Israel and one which taught students how to make Molotov cocktails. We immediately put out a press release ridiculing this idea: firstly, there was no such book. Secondly, students do not need to learn how to make a Molotov cocktail from a book. It's not a complex weapon like an atomic bomb.

The largest regular communal event took place on 30 March each year. In Palestine this is known as Land Day, and dates back to a very important event that occurred in 1976, when six Palestinians living in Galilee, inside Israel's borders, were killed by Israeli troops. They had been protesting in an entirely peaceful way against the confiscation of over 5,500 acres of land belonging to the Palestinian Arabs in the area. Afterwards, their land was used to settle Jews on, in an attempt to create a Jewish majority in a predominantly Arab area of Israel.

After a few years of demonstrating about this, we decided on a new approach: we would instead show that we really respected and protected the land by planting it. We had planted trees before, but this was to be a large-scale event. We prepared some 20,000 saplings which ranged in height between 50 cm and a metre. The trees had been chosen by Nazar Banayan, a friend of ours who is a landscaping expert, and we asked all students and staff to be present. We knew the Israelis would try to stop us.

Early on the morning of Land Day 1983, soldiers at the Abu Qash checkpoint tried to stop me from reaching the university. After a certain amount of dialogue, assertive but not impolite, I managed to convince them to allow me through. I had explained that the university was not currently closed by military order and I needed to get to my office. It was better for everybody if there was someone responsible present.

Although the army had closed all the roads leading to Birzeit University before dawn, I was pleased to see that staff and students were spread widely around the university, having made their way from a variety of distant locations.

Present too, or at least nearby, was the military governor, who wanted to know what we were doing. I explained that we were planting trees. His response was to ask: 'Do you have a permit?' I was aware that there was indeed a military order stating that no one was allowed to plant trees without a permit, even on their own land, but decided to wing it. I replied with a straight face: 'Of course we do,' and he, luckily, did not pursue the matter further.

This was one permit I was certainly never going to ask for: the trees were to be on our land and we needed no permission to put them there. We all now lined up to start the job, myself included. The students stood in a row starting at the bottom of the hill and reaching right up to the hill of the campus at the top. It was a beautiful sight: the students were forming a chain and the trees were passed from one person to the next, giving the optical illusion of a moving forest. It's a great shame none of us had a video camera to capture the scene.

All the activity took place under the watchful eyes of the military personnel stationed on the hill right opposite the campus. We could see them following our movements through a large telescope. I suggested that the military governor send us some copies of the pictures they were taking for our records. I don't think he was used to our kind of humour, but this was the kind of relationship I tried to foster with the military authorities. I did not show them disrespect, but I kept my own dignity and never displayed a submissive attitude. If I spoke to them, I did so as an equal.

At noon I told the officer that we needed to go to the old campus to prepare some lunch. After some argument, we managed to get through the army roadblock. We got into our pickup truck, collected the food prepared for 600 students and transported it to the hill, all under the watching eyes of the soldiers.

At midday, the military governor told me that there was a busload of Birzeit students stuck at Jifna, a small village near Birzeit. Apparently this group had found the checkpoint leading to the new campus closed, so they had taken the route through Jalazon Refugee Camp and Jifna. This way, they had hoped to reach the campus unnoticed but had unfortunately been detained. I drove to Jifna to negotiate with the soldiers, insisting that they release the people on the bus. After a while, they relented and the students were able to join the rest in planting trees.

It had been a highly effective project. We had not shown the soldiers that we were angry, just that we were determined. Planting trees was both a firm protest and a positive step. The Israeli military did not want Palestinians to plant trees. Planting the mountainside with trees would prevent the rainwater from flowing towards the coastal plains, where Israel benefits from our rainwater. Another reason, we believe, is even subtler: it simply reinforces the connection of the Palestinians with their land. Planting trees, even on your own land, needed a permit. We believed doing so was our duty and our right. We choose not to abide by the laws of the military government, but by humanitarian, environmental and international law instead. It was in devising such activities that Birzeit took the lead.

Most academics enjoy a quiet, contemplative life. My life, though, has been shaped by the force of the occupation. The experience has led me to feel that leading the life of an academic in the face of daily denials of your rights is not the way to peace and happiness. Such a response would be unnatural. As I see it, being thrown off your land and denied your freedom inevitably prompts an urge to resist. This has been true at all times and everywhere. The question which I have tried to resolve in my mind is: what are legitimate means of resistance?

The Executive Committee of the Council for Higher Education during their annual meeting, 1993

I am non-violent by nature, and my readings of history have shown me that violence breeds violence. This has led me to join an international organisation called the Pugwash Conferences on Science and World Affairs, Pugwash for short. Pugwash is inspired by the ideas of Bertrand Russell and Albert Einstein and seeks to bring together, from around the world, influential scholars and public figures concerned with reducing the danger of armed conflict and seeking cooperative solutions for global problems. Pugwash Conferences, which are held annually, are attended by 150 to 250 scientists and social scientists; the more frequent topical workshops and symposia typically involve 30 to 50 participants. A basic rule is that participation is always by individuals in their private capacity, not as representatives of governments or organisations. This, I feel, is the spiritual community to which I belong.

The first political leader to inspire me was Mahatma Gandhi. Self-government worth its name, he taught, could only be achieved through non-cooperation and a non-violent political struggle. Those who sought freedom had to stand firm in support of their ideas, but also act without hatred.

Another influence was Nelson Mandela. As a student protester, he had taken part in an attack on some racists, but he later emphasised that he 'had no love for violence', despite the racist brutality of the apartheid regime. This did not mean he was meek. When in jail and threatened by a warder to force him to obey a humiliating order, he had replied: 'If you so much as lay a hand on me, I will take you to the highest court in the land, and when I finish with you, you will be as poor as a church mouse.' In the struggle for freedom, it was crucial to keep one's principles and one's self-respect. 'Any man or institution that tries to rob me of my dignity will lose,' Mandela later wrote in notes smuggled out by friends.

I felt that this was the path which people seeking to build a decent future society should seek to follow. Non-violence is not necessarily the only strategy, but it is certainly the most important one.

So, when it came to building up Birzeit, I saw myself as carrying out a national project that I would not allow the Israelis to impede. Keeping the university going and producing new generations of knowledgeable, proud and tolerant young people has been a way of claiming our rights as a nation and as human beings. And, given the conditions in which we lived, letting the students voice their demands for change by demonstrating on campus or in the streets of their own community seemed legitimate to me too.

But the Israeli determination to destroy our university has radicalised many of our students. When a group of armed men at a checkpoint can trample on students' books, beat them up and prevent them from attending classes (at worst, by putting them in jail) the young victims will not take this lying down.

When carrying a placard naming a UN resolution which lays down your rights is enough to get you shot, then throwing stones at soldiers or settlers armed with M16s that can fire 100 bullets a minute may seem like a legitimate response. To argue that to throw stones is to be against peace, as apologists for Israel's policies do, is to miss the point. A military occupation is not a state of peace. Since 1967, when we in the occupied territories lost what was left of our sovereignty and our freedom, we have been looking for peace with justice. One might say that peace cannot be attained without justice, but I want to emphasise that we are not looking for absolute justice, but merely for justice as perceived by international law.

In any case, peace is more than the absence of war. This is necessary for peace, but not sufficient. When we talk about peace between nations or between people, the essential element is the acceptance of the other, not simply as another human being but as a person equal in every way. There has to be mutual respect. And can we ever gain respect without being treated as equals? I believe the answer is a definite 'no'.

It is here that education plays a major role. When people attain a higher level of education, they can communicate better with others and can therefore reach an understanding based on respect. It is with this idea in mind that our university was established. One of its key objectives was to educate young Palestinians for a future in which they could take their rightful place as respected citizens among the nations of the world. Education is a liberating factor, and attacks on it have always been a way of keeping down subjugated nations.

So university students who became victims of the occupation, unwittingly or by challenging it, knew they could count on us. The university ran a Prisoners Committee consisting of students and local and international academic staff. Our help was practical and humanitarian: as soon as a student was detained, the committee made sure they had his personal details and ID number so that lawyers could apply for an order seeking his release. Without this, he risked being tortured, expelled to Lebanon or Jordan or jailed.

That Israel's growing brutality has pushed some Palestinians to go beyond those forms of resistance pioneered in Birzeit is a sad but perhaps inevitable development. One of today's Palestinian leaders, Marwan Barghouti, whose studies at Birzeit were curtailed when he was forcibly expelled from the West Bank in 1987, embraced armed resistance on returning in 1994. After being jailed by the Israelis, he wrote in a January 2002 op-ed column in the *Washington Post*:

> Israel will have security only after the end of the occupation, not before. ... I am not a terrorist, but neither am I a pacifist. I am simply a regular guy from the Palestinian street advocating what every other oppressed person has advocated – the right to help myself in the absence of help from anywhere else.

Birzeit continues to teach students about non-violent routes to justice. Our experience – mine and my students' – of dealing with Israel's army has reinforced my beliefs. Over the years, I have observed the impact of violence and the devastation it can cause. Also, a violent action tends to achieve nothing more than triggering a violent reaction. As a result, I feel ever more strongly that I have chosen the right way when it comes to dealing with the occupation.

Resistance requires one to be clear about its means and ends. The Palestinian strategies adopted in the first intifada, in which young people confronted Israeli tanks, armoured cars and guns with little more than stones, was a relatively restrained response to Israeli violence. However, if the response to the students' peaceful demonstrations had not been so brutal, perhaps both sides would by now have found a way towards a political solution allowing both sides to co-exist in two states.

As we became more confident in our stand, we began to seek more formal links with universities in other countries. Academic treaties and twinning agreements, common among institutes of higher education, might be able to gain us recognition for our efforts. The general role of education in our people's lives needed to be internationally acknowledged. Establishing formal links that would reflect such ideas proved a challenging but rewarding project.

We were also, of course, aware that the closure of the university had met with a disappointingly low level of protest abroad, almost none at all. The closures could continue for so long, many of us felt, because Birzeit was a Palestinian institution, a domestic initiative by Palestinian people. It had accreditation and recognition as a centre of excellence, yet because we were Palestinians we had never quite got the attention, support or protection we deserved. There had been some of this, but never enough.

The reason for this was that Israel still managed to make the rules, defining whatever Palestinians did in its own deliberately misleading terms. Even worse, the Israelis had for decades denied the very existence of Palestine and the Palestinians.

We initially believed that relations with the universities of Europe were of the greatest importance. Not only were they geographically closest to us, but many of their students and staff already felt some sympathy for us. With this in mind, we pioneered regular exchange visits with groups of university professors from France, Belgium, the Netherlands, West Germany, Sweden and Britain. In England, we established a sister relationship with the University of Durham, through which graduate students from Birzeit would get a scholarship for postgraduate work at Durham. We also had students from Durham come to Birzeit and join the community work programme in summer.

Another result of these initiatives was a link-up with the University of Bremen in Germany. Having learned about our situation, Bremen offered us several scholarships for Palestinian students coming straight from high school. These proved only a qualified success. Palestinian students often struggled with the transition from Palestinian society and its education system to its German equivalent. Moreover, those who succeeded in making this transition tended to stay in Germany, which had not been the idea.

We then agreed with Bremen that the scholars it funded would complete their first degree at Birzeit University before attending postgraduate courses in Germany. This worked well and we still maintain excellent relations with the university. It is a young, rather left-wing institution concerned about the evils of racism. As a result, even those who criticised its links with us were unable to smear it as anti-Semitic.

We also built a good relationship with the University of Amsterdam (UvA). Some of its professors visited Birzeit and gave lectures there. Moreover, in the autumn of 1984 I was invited to sign a sistership agreement with UvA. After the signing ceremony, I gave a talk about Birzeit, followed by a question-and-answer session. As expected, there were some pro-Israeli, or even Israeli, students among the audience who tried to harass me and the rector by saying that this gesture was an indication of anti-Semitism.

The rector was very firm in his response. He stressed that UvA had a good relationship with the Hebrew University of Jerusalem and that it was entitled also to create academic ties with other universities such as Birzeit. At this, the Zionists among the audience moved on to claim that not only was Birzeit affiliated with the PLO but that its president was a member of the PLO Executive Committee. Since the PLO was considered a terrorist organisation, they argued, it followed that Birzeit was a 'terrorist' university. Fortunately, life under the Israeli occupation had supplied me with lots of examples and facts showing who was the terrorist and who the underdog.

When speaking abroad, we always had to prove that ours was a university in every sense of the word. Even educated audiences were often unaware that Palestinians were normal people with normal educational aspirations. We also tried to make clear that Birzeit was a Palestinian national university and that its ambition was to be free and to find itself in an independent Palestinian state alongside Israel. I always welcomed questions from the floor, especially by Zionists, as this gave me a chance to expose their lies about us.

The day after the signing of the Amsterdam agreement, Israel provided me with a very chilling example of the horrors wrought by the occupation. One of our staff phoned from Birzeit in a state of agitation to tell me about the killing of Sharaf At-Tibi, an engineering student from Gaza. The story of this student from Gaza, shot dead by Israeli soldiers during a peaceful demonstration, was picked up by the Dutch press. It was a painful confirmation of Israel's attitude to Palestinian education.

At Uppsala University in Sweden, two professors of theology, Jan Bergman and Sigbert Axelson, developed close ties with Birzeit. I was invited to the University of Uppsala and lectured there about our situation. I also met the rector of the university, who immediately told me about his friendship with, and support for, Israel. His family had been very active in saving the Jews during the Nazi occupation. As a result, he could not, unfortunately, fathom the idea that some Jews might no longer be victims but persecutors; he could see the Palestinians only as people who were denying the right of Israel to exist.

I tried to tell the rector what was really happening in Palestine, that we were not anti-Semitic but trying to free ourselves from a brutal occupation. It was a civil meeting but he, like others in Europe, seemed to have absorbed the propaganda line that Israelis were incapable of acts such as dispossession or occupation: they were just Jews trying to defend themselves in a sea of Arabs and their state was a bastion of democracy.

I came to accept that the mere existence of the Palestinians needed

The author heading the first Steering Committee meeting of the PEACE Programme at BZU, 1992

to be explained, even to academic audiences. This was largely for historic reasons: ever since the Balfour Declaration, we have been referred to in non-national terms, not as Palestinians but as 'the indigenous non-Jewish communities'. We were not supposed to have any 'national' feeling, as we were just a part of the Arab world. In fact, we were not supposed to exist. Under the British mandate, Palestinians were not allowed to have national representatives, but only religious community leaders (Christian and Muslim), which would be appointed by the British government. The Jewish leaders in Palestine, on the other hand, were treated as people representing a national entity.

The Palestinians' relationship with the Arab world also needed explaining. Naturally, we believed in the pan-Arab concept, as we all belonged to the greater Arab nation, but each country was a national entity. Palestinians are Arabs in the same way as Italians are Europeans. These categories are complementary, not mutually exclusive. (Of course, defining 'Jewishness' raises many more problems of categorisation.) In time, each Arab country came to develop its national traditions and pride in belonging to that nation, which in our case was Palestine.

So, audiences sometimes seemed to wonder, why had Palestine not prevailed over the attempts of European Zionists to take over their country? I had to make clear that our people were ill-prepared to fight such a well-organised, well-funded movement at all levels, technologically, educationally, economically and legally. It was also hard to grasp the full truth without actually seeing how we lived. We needed foreign visitors and witnesses. At the moment, Israeli propaganda was preventing the international community from taking the right decisions. However, this could not ultimately detract from the fact that we were entitled to be a free nation like all others. Our people were rebelling against colonial rule.

Nevertheless, many academics took an interest in our situation, as well as our academic work, and I gradually established ties with several of them, including the French Paris VII and Paris X Universities, as well as the Free University of Brussels (ULB) and the German Erlangen-Nürnberg University. The university that proved most helpful to us was Louvain-La-Neuve in Belgium.

My son happened to be studying at Louvain and I got to know the university's Head of International Relations, Simon-Pierre Nothomb, who was also the Secretary-General of the COIMBRA group, an association of long-established European universities. During the intifada, when all the Palestinian universities were closed by Israeli

The author signing a cooperation agreement with the president of Amsterdam University (left), 1984

military order, I made an urgent call to Nothomb and pleaded with him that the COIMBRA universities should do something to help us rather than simply look on, sitting on the fence. Sure enough, that June, he responded by bringing over to the country a delegation of senior COIMBRA figures. To my relief, we signed a collaboration agreement called PEACE (Palestinian European Academic Cooperation in Education) in the Notre Dame Centre in Jerusalem in 1991. The agreement offered scholarships to students from the closed Palestinian universities to join a similar course in one of the universities in the network. As the idea caught on, the PEACE programme was expanded to a network of over 40 European universities, five American universities and all eleven Palestinian universities. Staff mobility between the Palestinian and European partners was also encouraged for both teaching and joint research. The network continues to operate to this day and marks an important turning point in the relations between European and Palestinian universities.

Afterwards, we met with the Director General of UNESCO, and asked him for support. He gave us a modest sum but very important logistic and moral support. This encouraged European and leading American universities to join the programme. Birzeit now became part of the UNESCO University Twinning Programme, allowing us to hold the PEACE General Assembly meeting once every two years. As the presidency of the PEACE programme was at Birzeit University, the first General Assembly was hosted by our university in 1992. This coincided with Birzeit's student elections, in which well over 80 per cent of students took part. The university had just reopened after 51 months of military-ordered closure and I asked our computer centre, which was still in its infancy, to design a programme that would give us the election results straight after the students had voted. This was the first time in Palestine that an election of any sort had been computerised. The visitors were able to observe student democracy at work in Palestine, and Birzeit emerged as a pioneering body in this field.

During the meeting at Birzeit, the General Assembly of the PEACE programme decided that the next assembly meeting would be convened at the University of Louvain-La-Neuve, along with an international conference on education. The theme chosen during the Louvain meeting was 'Academic Cooperation with Palestinian Higher Education Institutions'.

UNESCO involvement increased when Dr Adnan Badran, who was the Deputy Director for Science of UNESCO, gave his support to the opening of a PEACE Programme office and an assistant to be established at UNESCO.

In 1978 there were efforts to persuade UNESCO to send a mission that would investigate Israeli violations in the field of education. Israel tried to block this in a variety of ways. Nevertheless, we started to prepare a report to be submitted to UNESCO in case the mission was allowed to come to the occupied Palestinian territories.

One April day in 1982, I received a call from the assistant military governor, Major Eli Tsur, asking me to come and see him in his Beit El office. Major Tsur was of Egyptian origin. He spoke Arabic with us and tried to be helpful. After the usual exchanges, he asked me whether I knew why he had invited me. I was wondering what the answer might be, hoping that it was not some bad news, as life was currently quiet at the university. Tsur explained that UNESCO officials had asked to see me and he was to take me to Jerusalem to meet with them. That was an unpleasant surprise. I responded angrily that we had been expecting the UNESCO team for some time. They were supposed to visit us at Birzeit. I refused to go to Jerusalem, explaining that there was no point in meeting them unless I could bring the report we had prepared. The major suggested that I call the university and have them send me the report, but I preferred to go back myself, collect it and return. Once I'd done that, Tsur took me in his car to the Moriah Hotel in Jerusalem.

It was strange to be taken almost clandestinely to Jerusalem in order to meet the UNESCO team. When we arrived, the only person present was a Yugoslav member of the team, who said that the rest had gone to the Allenby Bridge. I did not know whether to laugh or cry. I could not understand why a UNESCO team coming to report on the status of education in the occupied Palestinian territories would travel to the Allenby Bridge, apparently in order to report how Israel was allowing people to cross the bridge in a 'civilised' manner

The Yugoslav told me that he had been left behind in Jerusalem because he was not feeling well. We were talking in front of the military officer and when the UNESCO envoy started asking questions, I commented ironically that one example of our freedom as Palestinians was that I could not talk with him except in the presence of a military officer. The Israeli officer reacted by offering to leave if we wanted him to. I replied that he could stay. I had no secrets and wanted him to hear what I was saying, hoping it would open his eyes to reality. I had made my point anyway.

I first mentioned the issue of journals. We had been denied a permit by the Israeli authorities to receive journals from Arab countries. Even though the list we submitted contained only journals freely available at the Hebrew University, we were denied a permit to get them on subscription. The major listening in now interrupted to say that we could submit the list if we wanted. This was not a problem, he said, he would handle the journal issue himself.

When Tsur left the room I continued talking to the UNESCO envoy about life under occupation, the closures and the denial of access to education. I then asked him what had happened to the rest of the team. He told me that soldiers were accompanying the UNESCO team all the time and would not leave them for a minute. When the team had asked to go to Birzeit University, they were told that their security would be at risk. This is why they had been taken to the Allenby Bridge instead.

The man had decided to stay behind to meet me by claiming to be sick. I offered to take him to Birzeit, but he replied that the team's 'guardians' might make this difficult. However, he suggested that he and the rest of the UNESCO team might be able to meet us during one of their evenings off.

Cheered by this plan, I arranged for a Jerusalem taxi to pick them up so that whoever was watching the team's movements would not suspect anything. The driver then brought the team to Birzeit where we had gathered several university professors and we had a lively discussion with them about the situation, which lasted most of the evening. Of course, we also handed over the report we had prepared for them.

I did not forget what the Israeli officer had said about the journals. The next day I submitted my list to him, asking for a permit. There was no response, so I called him about the matter. Tsur asked for the list to be sent again. A month passed and we did not receive the permit. I contacted him and again he asked me for the list. After sending it more than four times, I asked furiously if he was starting a collection of these lists. Time went by, and we were never granted a permit for the journals.

This is one of the many examples of Israelis saying one thing in public while doing something quite different beyond the glare of publicity. Our problem is that once a pronouncement is made, people assume that something has actually been done. It can take ages to correct this impression.

As for the report the UNESCO team produced after their visit, it was never published, having been attacked by friends of Israel as anti-Semitic. In it, the team had criticised Israel because they had been prevented from going off and seeing the status of schools without being escorted by officers in a jeep. It was easy to imagine what kind of statements the school teachers would haven given in such circumstances, as all were government employees and answerable to the Israeli education officer at the end of the day

A second UNESCO mission, headed by Father E. Bonét, a professor at the University of Louvain, arrived in 1987. This time we managed to take the team to the campus to see how things stood. It was during the intifada and the campus was closed. This report, too, was not published. It became part of UNESCO archives but no action resulted from its condemnation of Israel's military policies.

9

NETWORKING ROUND THE WORLD

How effective were our efforts to gather international support? This is a complex question and the answer is mainly guesswork. Networking was clearly worthwhile. The relationships we developed with universities in Europe and the United States have been useful to us and to our students on the academic level. These universities were our window to the outside world. Contact with them gave us the opportunity to assess our academic achievements as some of our students went on to these universities. It also allowed our staff to meet with academic colleagues there. In addition, such collaboration exposed our students to other cultures and different perspectives, which is a key aspect of university education.

The networking also enabled us to paint a truthful picture about the occupation in Palestine and expose the serious violations taking place under the guise of 'security' and the well-publicised allegedly 'benign occupation'.

As for the closures, external intervention never caused the Israelis to rescind a closure order when the order was for a limited period of time (one week, one or two months, etc). However, when the closures were for an indefinite period, outside pressure tended to be effective. But when information about the closure of a university was publicised in the international media, Israel often tried to reduce the impact of this by telling lies and by providing false information or half-truths about the reason for the closure.

Israel likes to present itself as the champion of academic freedom everywhere. This stance is the basis for its public criticism of the growing international movement for an academic boycott of Israeli universities. So any publicity that tarnishes this image is unwelcome, and Israel's representatives will try hard to dismiss it. However, we managed to reduce the impact of the closures by publicising the severity of the Israeli actions. While a one-month closure is bad enough, being closed for two months would have been even worse.

Parliamentary links certainly had an impact. Our major support in the European Parliament came from members who had good links with our solidarity groups. We told them about our extreme frustration at the lack of action by European governments against Israeli practices in the occupied territories and their violations of the Geneva Convention, which forbids the closure of universities.

We also mentioned a meeting we had held with the Consular Corps. This is the group of consuls general in Jerusalem that existed prior to 1967 and were taking care directly of the Palestinians in the occupied territories without referring to their embassies in Tel-Aviv: American, British, French, Spanish, Italian, Greek, Turkish and Swedish. This meeting included the Italian foreign minister, who had visited the country soon after the first intifada. The strong protests the consuls sent to Israel then had, so we told them, ended up in the wastepaper bin. Therefore, if the parliamentarians were serious about human rights, they needed to take stronger steps. They could, for instance, freeze the agreements they had with Israeli universities in the fields of research and cooperation until Israel reopened the Palestinian universities. Sure enough, the subject was brought up in the European parliament and the decision was taken to freeze this cooperation agreement in 1990.

It is hard to say whether it was our pleas, the work of the parliamentarians or the international situation which produced this result, but it was important. Israel was furious and did not want to appear to be giving in to pressure. However, soon after this decision, Bethlehem University was re-opened. As usual, Israel publicised this fact, but implied that all the universities were now open, by lumping all educational institutions together. Palestinian primary and secondary schools were often closed during the intifada, so whenever they were re-opened Israel would announce that everything was now open. This would make people abroad think that the statement also referred to universities.

Unfortunately, the Gulf War broke out the next year and this led to the resumption of the research cooperation agreement with Israel. The Israelis eventually announced that they would be opening the universities gradually after the opening of Bethlehem University, but it took them another three years to allow Birzeit, the last one, to open. Had it not been for the Gulf War, I believe, the action of the EU Parliament would have borne fruit much faster.

In the United States we had limited success, simply because the Israel lobby was omnipresent. Whenever we did have a breakthrough with Congress thanks to the help of one or two congressmen, Israel and its lobby group would swamp the Congress and Senate with packages of misinformation and half-truths which countered our efforts. We had neither the time nor the money to continue fighting this kind of misrepresentation (see Appendix III and Appendix IV representing Israeli statements and our rebuttals respectively).

In recent years, US willingness to support Palestinians, in material terms at least, has improved considerably. However, we are concerned about the strings often attached to funding offers. Money for Palestinian educational activities is increasingly tied to cooperation with Israeli academic institutions. Many US (and even some European) grant-giving bodies will offer funds to Palestinian universities only for projects which also involve Israelis. This is seen as promoting peace and understanding by the donors, but actually humiliates the potential Palestinian recipients without any real advancement towards peace.

What donors fail to understand is that we will only cooperate on a basis of equality. Why should we want to sit alongside Israeli academics while we are hampered by Israel in our academic work and cannot even travel freely for academic purposes? Why should we pretend that doing academic work together in the current situation represents some sort of normality? All that this kind of cooperation does is make Israelis feel good.

As the Dean of Birzeit's Faculty of Graduate Studies, Dr Lisa Taraki, has put it:

> Luring fund-starved Palestinian academics in such a manner can be seen as a form of political blackmail, regardless of the intentions of sponsors. We believe that if international funding institutions are sincere about their intentions of developing the scientific and research capacity of Palestinian institutions and scholars, they should offer direct assistance and not politicise their support.

During the first intifada, the Jordanian dinar was devalued to half its value in 1988. This had a very negative impact on our staff salaries, which were based on the dinar. The universities had to work out a new pay scale taking this devaluation into consideration. Our financial problems were further compounded when the PLO was not able to fulfil its obligations after the Gulf War.

The resulting money shortages at times put a strain on relations between administrative and teaching staff at the universities. At the national level, we always formed a united front vis-à-vis Israeli rights violations and actions against the Palestinians in general and the university in particular. However, when it came to financial matters the situation was different. Staff unions and university leaders often found themselves at loggerheads over limited resources.

Like our students, the Birzeit Staff and Faculty Union has passed through different stages, always with the idea of open discourse and freedom of expression. When the college was small, relations were very informal and in Birzeit we never lacked the means of discourse.

But as the college turned into a university with larger numbers of students and staff, the need arose for more effective organisation and unionisation, not just for dealing with the university administration but also for national and organisational reasons. The staff and faculty unions merged and later amalgamated with other unions, finally forming the Association of Staff and Faculty Unions at the Palestinian Universities, which had an office at An-Najah National University.

While I could understand the reasons behind this arrangement and the financial demands it led to, I was not very happy. My view of university staff unions had initially been rather utopian: I always thought and acted as if we were all one body with two major goals in common: the quality of services we were giving to students and our national need to get rid of occupation.

I now worried that such unions might drive a wedge between the staff on the one hand and university leaders on the other. I was also concerned about a politicisation of the union. Rather than working for a broad national agenda, I feared that we would slide into factional politics, where the common interest of the university might lose out to power struggles and special interests. This, in turn, could lead to polarisation and a lack of general unity.

While none of my worries turned out to be entirely justified, the constant shortage of university funds remained potentially divisive. The root of the shortage was our complex funding structure. In the late 1980s, the issue of finances was generally worked out collectively between the Council for Higher Education (CHE) – the body that secured funding for the universities' running costs – and the Association of University Unions, and that included the setting of a unified salary scale for all university employees.

While student fees formed part of our income, our main source was grants from external donors and from the Arab countries, channelled through the PLO. Some staff somehow came to believe that the university was getting funds but not divulging the information, which of course was not true since we had to account transparently to our donors. In fact, the staff were mixing up funds earmarked for building purposes, which we had been successful in raising, mostly through the efforts of Hanna Nasir with the help of the board of the university, and funds for running costs, which were always hard to obtain.

This confusion prompted a number of strikes. Whenever one of those took place, the non-academic staff got the better part of the deal, since the strike days were not generally recouped. The academic staff, on the other hand, had to make up for lost days by working Fridays or Sundays, or extending the academic year in cases of long strikes.

On one occasion, when funds were particularly short, Birzeit staff held a major strike. The PLO had asked us through the CHE to reduce staff salaries so as to meet our costs, rather than increase the fees, which was not an option the PLO would consider. The university leadership would not back down and the strike lasted almost three months. It ended in a compromise based on the principle that the salary cut would be considered a one-time donation to the university. It was the kind of year that I hope will never be repeated at any university.

After the establishment of the Palestinian National Authority in 1994, following the Oslo Accords, the Council for Higher Education under the Ministry for Education and Higher Education continued to handle the negotiations with the unions over living costs and the salary-scale changes.

Funding, however, continues to be a hot issue. Without adequate funding, the Palestinian universities cannot provide the staff and administration necessary for high-class tertiary education, however much they might like to improve staff salaries. Hanna Nasir used to say that this was a financial problem and as such had to be solved financially. However, this does not make life any easier for Palestinian university leaders. They may be sympathetic, but in the final analysis the problem cannot be solved to the entire satisfaction of the staff unions. Under the prevailing conditions everybody, including the unions, may need to understand and compromise until the situation improves.

One of the proposed solutions to the financial crisis was to set up an endowment fund for the universities, to be held by the Council for Higher Education. This would have ensured that we had regular funding to cover any deficits. Unfortunately, such a fund has never been set up.

To improve our funding situation, the Palestinian Council for Higher Education decided to apply to the EEC (later the EU) for funding. We had seen how supportive they had been over the issue of closures, when they passed a resolution supporting the re-opening of the universities and freezing the cooperation agreement with the Israelis. But when we approached the EEC this time, the answer was that the organisation could not pay for running costs. So we had to prepare a project that would help us support the running costs of the universities and at the same time fit within the EEC criteria. What we came up with was 'Off Campus Teaching' a project in which the EEC could cover the cost of housing students who could not move from their towns and villages to their universities, as well as the cost of teachers, transportation and sundries. We were able to obtain close to $800,000 for the universities, which was a lifesaver.

Our contacts with the EU also established the Council for Higher Education as the body representing Palestinian higher education institutions and accredited to receive funds from the EU for the following five years. We then submitted and gained funds for a second project, aimed at upgrading the qualifications of high-school teachers. After the Oslo Accords, we began to receive direct funding from the EU to cover staff salaries at the universities, relieving the Palestine National Authority of this burden.

While submitting new projects, we also tried to press the PLO for funding. This was arriving in only minute quantities and we had accumulated debts. The universities were advised to draw instead on their provident funds or compensation funds so they could admit new students. 'Provident funds' are a kind of a saving scheme where a certain percentage, say 5 per cent, of the monthly salary of the employee is set aside and the university adds 10 per cent. The total is then invested for the benefit of the employee, who takes the whole sum upon retirement or leaving the university. 'Compensation funds' are stipulated in the labour law but the university improved on this law by paying the employee upon retirement, or at the end of his/her contract, the equivalent of one month of final salary for each year of employment. This is over and above the provident fund. These two funds were managed by the university. Birzeit indeed did this, but younger universities, which did not have such funds, simply stopped paying salaries, putting the payment on account.

As a result, employees of certain universities had a salary backlog equivalent to nine to twelve months, so for four or five years they

The author and colleagues with Sir Anthony Nutting during his visit to Birzeit University, 1982

were only receiving half their pay. In addition, it was decided during the uprising that students would not pay fees. Now, as soon as some of the universities started opening, we agreed that those universities had to start charging fees.

Establishing unified pay scales based on the new, lower value of the Jordanian dinar was another challenge. This took a lot of haggling between the staff and the unions on one side, and the university administration and the board of trustees on the other. The latter were worried that this new scale, which had a similar buying power to the old one, would burden them with financial obligations they could ill afford.

As the universities were ultimately paying, their leaders insisted that if they were to implement the pay scale, the Council had to guarantee that it would cover the added expense on the part of the universities. Unfortunately, a series of problems, including the Gulf War and its aftermath, prevented this from happening. The Council, moreover, was not a funding agency, but rather a channel for funds.

Fortunately, some Palestinian businessmen donated funds to individual universities. One donor, Mr Sabih El Masri, paid the Council $300,000 a month for two years to help cover the running costs of the universities.

Some of the universities, mainly the older and more prestigious ones like Birzeit, felt that if they had to raise staff salaries in line with all other universities, they should also be allowed to charge higher tuition fees because they were offering better services. The other universities argued that if you unify the salary scale, you also unify the fees.

Naturally, if you charge the same fees but offer more services (and your teacher-to-student ratio is different), then your university will have less money. That meant that universities offering poorer-quality education were proportionately receiving more fee support than universities such as Birzeit. Universities also sometimes chose to increase their class sizes so as to earn more money from fees. Unfortunately, this came at the expense of the quality of education.

All these issues gradually came to a head and led to arguments and strikes, which continue until the present day. Students demand lower fees or at least a freeze on fee increases. University employees, through their unions, demand higher salaries and improved pay scales. These two demands are often incompatible. Without constant support (in our case from our national body, the PLO), they certainly cannot be met.

After five years of intifada, we had to acknowledge that our national goal, an independent Palestinian state and Israel's acknowledgement of the rights of our refugees, was no nearer. However, the oppression of Palestinians by Israel had caught the attention of the world.

It had also shifted the outlook of some Israelis, including that of Brigadier Binyamin Ben Eliezer, the former head of the Israeli military government. Now a minister in an Israeli Labour government, 'Fuad' warned in the Israeli weekly *Koteret Rashit* in December 1987 that the Palestinians had changed, their young people were more educated, more confident and less likely to submit to military rule. 'They wear jeans, t-shirts and Adidas shoes and have university degrees,' he wrote. 'They are light-years removed from the previous generation.' What Israelis were seeing, he said, was 'the hatred of a frustrated society that has lost hope'.

We now saw ourselves as a political entity. In 1988, we declared a Palestinian state and in 1989 Palestinian leaders first spoke to Israelis. At the Madrid talks in 1991, the core of the Palestinian negotiating team was made up of Birzeit academics and Birzeit graduates. Israeli journalists quipped that Israel was actually negotiating for peace with Birzeit. Life was rapidly improving, though education was not, especially in our schools.

During the first intifada, schools had been closed for six months, and during the following year, 1988–89, the schools were again closed for a month or two. In 1989 we admitted around six or seven hundred students to Birzeit. This was a large number at that time. We started worrying about this for two reasons: first of all, because we now had a higher number of students than before, and because students who had completed their schooling during the intifada had not had enough preparation, so they came ill-prepared for university work.

We set up committees to explore what kinds of programmes they needed and devised a remedial programme including pre-admission reading materials. We also devised handouts and courses for the students. Entrance exams were introduced that were not so much aptitude tests as achievement examinations. For science students there were tests in maths and physics and in the arts there were tests in language and social sciences.

Some schools had taught for fewer than 30 days a year. Despite this, the military governor issued an order which stated that he considered the school year completed regardless of the number of teaching days. Jordanian law had stated clearly that no school year would be complete unless the requisite number of teaching days (210 for a six-day teaching week and 180 for a five-day one) had been reached. Some UNRWA schools had taught for far shorter periods, since they were quite often closed. Sometimes this was because the refugee camps were under curfew and at other times because the children were forbidden to go into the schools as a collective punishment.

When an academic year was not completed by the required time according to the academic calendar, schools would normally have extended the school year into the summer holidays. The schools preferred this to carrying over the syllabus into the next year, but the military governor did not allow it. Nor did he allow them to teach the remaining material in the following year.

In other words, the academic year could be defined as completed, regardless of the number of teaching days, and so students would start the following year with the material of the next grade, thus accumulating ignorance upon ignorance. Surveys conducted two or three years later showed that students in Grade Four were unable to read or write because when they had been in Grade One they had had little time to learn. Then, in Grade

Two, they had been made to start on new material without any catch-up teaching.

It was a sign of how far Israel's aims had come from conventional military needs that one of the tasks of Israel's military governors was to define such non-military factors as the length and nature of the school year in the territory they were occupying illegally. I believe this behaviour to be an actual crime and whoever was responsible for closing schools and universities (but especially schools) should be tried for committing a war crime against Palestinians. We ended up with generations of illiterates, which may well have been the intention.

Many of our new students had been in ninth or tenth grade when the intifada started. Teaching during its last five years had been very patchy and they lacked knowledge. While they were motivated to go to university, they were unprepared for it. The university had to bridge a huge gap. Despite our work, these students had a lot of problems academically. It took several years before we overcame the bad effects. Luckily, education is now in the hands of the Palestinians so that we can decide when a school year is over. Teachers have more flexibility in the way they handle their material and we are getting better-qualified teachers.

The Israelis, of course, did not care about the education of our children. When they controlled the schools, they did not like hiring university graduates as teachers and as a result the quality of education suffered.

Until 1992, the minimum qualification for primary school teachers was a teacher-training diploma after a two-year course. However, secondary school teachers needed a BA. The Israeli military government did not cooperate with the universities to allow university students who were doing teacher training to gain practical experience at government schools. We were left with only private schools for such training, of which there were few. Since universities were labelled by the Israelis as 'hotbeds of anti-Israeli sentiments' they preferred to employ the graduates of two-year college courses, who were more manageable. They were also less expensive.

As a result, many teachers struggled with the more demanding material taught to the senior pupils. They did not have enough subject knowledge. Even teachers with a university degree were often teaching in a field outside their specialisation. That was a particular problem when it came to subjects like chemistry or physics.

We started getting involved in remedial teaching during the first intifada, when we helped pupils to catch up by running classes in each area or quarter. Every street would have a committee which would help the students in that area to work through material that had been prepared in their school. UNRWA, the Friends' schools and other private schools provided complete teaching packages.

During the intifada, we also conducted workshops in which we trained teachers to teach under abnormal conditions of closure. If a government school was closed, we sometimes tried to place its students in another school so they had an opportunity to learn. Some university students would tutor pupils in clandestine classes. This was punishable by ten years imprisonment under Israeli military law, and some students were actually charged and given such draconian sentences for teaching high-school kids.

The military also defined as a crime the provision of teaching packages by UNRWA. After all, the closure order was not a proper punishment if students were still able to study. It is ironic that while all kinds of real crimes were committed by the Israeli army, providing teaching materials for Palestinian children was considered illegal.

While Birzeit staff and students have always been united in their commitment to Palestinian nationhood and opposition to occupation, it was inevitable that world events would create differences in their wider views. After the overthrow of the Shah of Iran in 1979, people in Palestine came to identify with the Islamic revolution that had overthrown him. It was seen as a movement of the poor and weak which was resisting the huge US power behind the Shah's regime. Palestinians felt they were in a similar position to that of the Iranians, in that they were fighting an Israeli war machine supported by the United States. Khomeini's struggle for power was seen as inspiring.

At first Christians and Muslims alike sympathised with Khomeini's revolution. However, the euphoria soon ended. As more details about life in Iran emerged, it became clear to most of us that the revolutionaries had created an oppressive regime.

The Islamist groups in Palestine, though, continued to regard Iran as a role model. All they cared about was that the Islamic Revolution there had established Shari'a rule. At first, these groups were encouraged by Israel in order to weaken the PLO and all other resistance movements. On one occasion, the Islamic Brotherhood (the precursor of Hamas) was demonstrating in the streets of Gaza when its leaders decided to go further: they marched on the local Red Crescent Society and burnt it down. There was an Israeli army presence there, but its soldiers did not intervene. They knew that the Red Crescent was vaguely associated with the Communist Party, which was pro-resistance, and that Hamas was also against the Palestinian nationalist movements.

So Hamas was, directly or indirectly, always supported by Israel. We were quite aware that this was going on, and it turned out to be a mistake in the long run. Later, of course, the Americans would make the same mistake by supporting the Islamist Taliban in Afghanistan. Today, both the Israelis and the Americans are reaping the fruits of these decisions. As far as Israel was concerned at the time, though, the Islamic groups were doing exactly what it wanted. They were fighting the nationalist groups.

Birzeit, which always reflected what was going on in the rest of occupied Palestine, had a student body that was 25 per cent Islamist. This created tension with the rest of the student community, who viewed the Islamist groups as anti-nationalist. Birzeit was a nationalist university in the broad sense. Its students held a variety of views and supported political parties ranging from the left to the right. However, they all shared the view held by the majority of Palestinians that the PLO was the official and sole representative of the Palestinian people.

The Islamist movements did not recognise the PLO and instead fought for a future in which people would be ruled by an 'emir' (Islamic leader). This was blasphemy in many students' eyes. Even many of those who were devout Muslims could not accept the Islamists' stand.

On one occasion in 1983, the Islamist students planned an activity that had not been authorised by the Student Council, which was made up of nationalist factions. Coming from the direction of the mosque in the town of Birzeit, the Islamists marched with their green banners and janazir (chains) towards the western gate of the Old Campus. However, nationalist student groups were waiting for them and a clash ensued. In the end, the Islamist group was surrounded and we intervened, as we feared that a bitter fight might take place which would end badly.

I finally convinced the Student Council to stop the fighting and to let me try to work an 'armistice' so that we could evacuate the Islamist students from the building and get them back to the mosque by bus, unharmed. To make sure this would happen, I myself got them out and stayed with them for their protection in case any of the other students might restart the fight. This created a separation of forces and calm was restored, for the time being.

However, the problem of inter-student conflict had not been

resolved. Tension was still in the air and we felt that the only way to restore calm was to suspend classes and send the boarding students home until further notice. We needed to let the young hotheads cool down. As there was just one month left till the end of the term, the board of trustees met in an emergency session and decided to close the university for that time. The students were told to present themselves at the end of this period for their final examinations. It was the first time the university had been closed by an administrative rather than a military order.

We then took disciplinary measures by suspending the students responsible for starting the violence and set up committees to investigate the matter. Dignitaries from Gaza to Jerusalem tried to exert pressure on the university administration and on its board of trustees. Dealing with all this was a time-consuming process and often very tense, but we stood firm. Most importantly, we were speaking with one voice.

Pro-Jordanian forces also wanted to commission a report, as they felt that the university had dealt unfairly with the Islamist groups. A delegation came to investigate the matter. Irritatingly, the secular nature of the university was interpreted as an act against Islam. No one mentioned the Israeli role in creating tensions between the Islamist groups and the PLO.

Another incident took place on the new campus in the spring of 1986. This time it involved Fateh and the PFLP (Popular Front for the Liberation of Palestine). Students from Bethlehem University (who were mainly PFLP supporters) had been invited to an activity organised by the Front in Birzeit. Fateh students tried to stop them and soon a fight broke out. Stones and blocks were hurled from the rooftops by both sides and glass from the windowpanes was scattered all over. The fight caused substantial damage to our buildings. Fighting even took place at the new library, whose shelves had just been installed. Fortunately, no books had yet been moved from the old one.

The Israeli army passed by, but did not intervene. I suspect they enjoyed what they saw. As I tried to stop the fight, I could see stones being thrown in both directions and flying over my head.

There was considerable community pressure to resolve this conflict. We brought together the heads of these two factions, including Faisal Husseini and others, but this had no effect. None of the student leaders wanted to stop fighting because this would make it look as if they had lost the battle. The fading of daylight solved the problem instead. Fighting gradually stopped as there is no way of throwing stones accurately in the dark.

Again, we had to take disciplinary measures and some students were suspended, while others received a warning notice. As before, we had to withstand a significant amount of community pressure in order to carry out the decisions of the disciplinary committee.

In the third year of Birzeit's closure during the intifada, Saddam Hussein committed his big blunder by occupying Kuwait and threatening to use chemical weapons. Palestinians had mixed feelings about this. We could not, by and large, accept the occupation of Kuwait. But Yasser Arafat was in a difficult situation. He had good relations with Iraq which, as we knew, was the Arab country which had most consistently supported the Palestinians. He also maintained good relations with the Kuwaitis.

Faced with this dilemma, the PLO leader tried to deal with the crisis in an amicable fashion. When he met Saddam he hugged him, which was one of his habits. People who saw him doing this on TV joked that he was whispering to Saddam to leave Kuwait. The hug had not been anything unusual, but was interpreted as an act of solidarity with Saddam Hussein. It was, however, to have very bad consequences for Palestinians in Kuwait, a prosperous, well-established community which had helped to build the country.

It was a confusing situation for people in the occupied Palestinian territories. While many Palestinians appreciated Saddam's consistent support for the Palestinians and his strong stand against those Western countries which had most actively supported Israel, they were concerned about their fellow nationals in occupied Kuwait.

Birzeit's academic staff was as divided as the students about the occupation of Kuwait by Iraq. However, there was a feeling among the public that while Arab countries like Saudi Arabia and Kuwait had made sweeping statements in favour of the Palestinians, Saddam was doing more. Some Palestinians stayed in Kuwait and tried to help the Kuwaitis during the occupation, while others there did not take any stand in the Gulf crisis.

When the Iraqis marched into Kuwait, the Palestinians there had of course been very scared. Iraqi soldiers did not distinguish between different inhabitants of the country. Later, Saddam tried to drive a wedge between Kuwaitis and non-Kuwaitis, who were mostly Palestinians. The problem was that the Palestinians there, whatever their views, had nowhere to go. They had to stay on. With the Iraqi occupation of Kuwait in place, they had to find a way to survive.

If Palestinians had been allowed to join the Kuwaiti army, I am sure many would have done so. They were after all defending their own homes and businesses. However, Palestinians were considered foreigners by Kuwait and not allowed to serve. Even those born in Kuwait were not given a Kuwaiti passport, just an annually renewable residence permit.

At the time of the invasion, many Palestinians resident in Kuwait were away on their summer vacation. When Saddam was expelled from Kuwait, none was allowed back, even if they had friends or business partners there. The Kuwaitis decided to get rid of all Palestinians once and for all. Some of our academic friends like Dr Ibrahim (who was the President of Kuwait University at the time, and later became our Minister of Education) were very bitter about this. I think they expected people here to support them vocally and to denounce what Arafat had done.

Taking such a line was not easy for Palestinians. Although some people did, and others argued that Abu Ammar had made a mistake, most did not want to get involved in any argument. The PLO was considered our national leadership and so any criticism of it in this matter was only voiced in private.

Apparently, Arafat had tried to mediate between Saddam and the other Arab states, especially Egypt, so as to forestall US intervention. There is said to have been a meeting between Arafat and King Fahed after the invasion and before the US attack, some time in November 1990. King Fahed was convinced that Arafat was right to try and solve the conflict in this way, but added that it was too late because the American army had started to come into Arabia and he could not say 'no' to the Americans. Once the Americans had entered Kuwait, it was all over. The US army was like a steamroller that kept on going, and there was no way to stop it.

In fact, Arafat's position at this point was no different from that taken by King Hussein. He too had been against the Iraqi invasion of Kuwait but also against letting any foreign forces interfere. In other words, the issue should be resolved internally between the Arab States. This position was denounced because it looked like neutrality, and anything that was not 100 per cent against Saddam was not accepted by the world.

It must be added that while there were many Palestinians in Kuwait, there was also a large battalion of Palestinian soldiers in Iraq. When the Palestinian army was dispersed in 1948, its fighters had mainly gone to Syria, Lebanon, Egypt and Tunisia. Some, though, had ended up in Iraq. We also had to take into consideration the safety of those people. They were like hostages.

So it was not easy for Palestinians to take a stand against either party. We wanted to protect the Palestinians in Kuwait and the Palestinians in Iraq. In other words, Palestinians were damned if they did and damned if they did not. As a result, many chose to remain neutral. While it was considered all right to be neutral on Saddam, being neutral about Kuwait was not. It may have looked as if we were backing Saddam, but most of us we were not.

The first Gulf War was a sad and ugly period of time for Palestinians, and the results are still with us. Many of the Palestinians in Kuwait had been the sole breadwinners of West Bank families. Once expelled, they had to be supported by their relatives here, rather than being able to support them.

Our reaction was to say that we were against all forms of occupation. We felt that the international community, which was so against the occupation of Kuwait by Saddam, should also object to the occupation of Palestine by Israel – if it wanted to be consistent.

When Saddam started threatening to use poisonous gas, Israel started distributing gas masks to its population. Some Palestinians in the West Bank felt that they were also in danger from such poisons. People were panicking and prepared sealed rooms with all kinds of provisions. We were unclear how this should be handled. People with small children were particularly worried.

When Saddam started firing his Scud missiles, we initially hid in our rooms as soon as we heard the radio sirens. Later some Palestinians took to watching the missiles from their roofs instead of being stuck in sealed rooms. They were rewarded with fascinating sights. The Scuds would move across the sky like shooting stars as they turned westward towards Tel Aviv. American Patriot anti-missile missiles would then try to stop them, but invariably failed.

After so many years of an unequal conflict in which they were not really able to hit back, people here liked seeing this. It was as if Israel was at last being made to take its own bitter medicine. Most Palestinians did not rejoice in the possibility that Israelis would be killed; what they hoped was that perhaps these events would open their opponents' eyes, give Israelis a sense of the fear, humiliation and destruction of property we were facing day by day. Unfortunately, I do not think the Israeli government or the majority of its people got that message.

We were kept under curfew for 40 days during the Gulf War. The soldiers would lift it at different times for two to three hours every few days. It was a scary period but, looking on the bright side, the curfew brought people together. Haifa and I would sneak from one house to another, making sure there was no army around. Our children were not in the country, so we were not as worried as other people. This brought us closer to our neighbours and friends like Salim and his wife Su'ad. She would later write an excellent book about their experiences, called *Sharon and My Mother-in-Law*.

We all would spend hours chatting, laughing and making fun of the situation. Humour was a way of reducing the tension. We would joke about the Israeli military reporter Nahman Shai who would announce the Scud missiles, mocking his mannerisms as well as his name, which in Arabic means tea. We used to say: 'Now it's time for coffee and tea!'

Another positive thing was that for the whole 40 days curfew, teaching did not stop. We managed to pass the exam sheets to students in Gaza, Bethlehem and elsewhere. This was an amazing achievement given the length of the closure.

Soon, initiatives were launched to resolve the situation in the Gulf. Strict measures were taken against Iraq for occupying Kuwait. Maybe the international community was also embarrassed about having ignored the Israeli occupation, as we witnessed a definite growth in international support for the Palestinians in the occupied territories. Our university community was fully involved in establishing landmarks for conflict resolution.

Following American intervention, the Madrid talks were initiated in 1989. We took great satisfaction from the fact that the Palestinian delegation to the talks was drawn mostly from Birzeit, a university which had been dismissed and persecuted as an alleged centre for anti-Israeli violence and which had suffered enormously from military control (see Appendix VIII – Letter to Secretary Baker).

The vice-chairman of the Palestinian delegation at Madrid, Nabeel Kassis, its spokesperson Hanan Ashrawi, and its press attaché Albert Aghazarian were all from Birzeit University. We had a vision for a comprehensive peace based on justice and the implementation of international law and UN resolutions.

This phase ended in the 1993 Oslo Agreement. That was the beginning of a new era. I cannot say if it was better or worse, but it was certainly different. There were people who believed from the very beginning that Oslo was a sell-out of the Palestinians. We had negotiated with the Israelis and recognised them as a state, they said, but we emerged without a state of our own, without freedom.

Still, I personally wanted to believe that Oslo had the potential to give us back our country, or at least produce an Israeli withdrawal from the Palestinian territories occupied in 1967. Even when the negotiations left the issue of the settlements unresolved, I was still optimistic that we might use these talks to have a sovereign Palestinian state alongside Israel, to dismantle the settlements and to implement the right of return of the Palestinian refugees. People were full of hope for development and statehood. Students, they believed, would now have a good chance of being employed in their own country rather than having to look for employment elsewhere. All these things led to tremendous optimism.

Israel had indeed ceded something at Oslo. Its forces now withdrew from the main Palestinian population centres. As soldiers left each city, people were elated and welcomed the Palestinian Authority. Around that time, Hanna Nasir returned from exile. His wife Tania recalls how she accompanied him the next day to the offices of the Ramallah's military governor to collect his ID. When a soldier brought out Hanna's file and opened it, Tania looked at her husband's picture there and burst into tears. He had been a young man when he was expelled. Now he was white-haired.

At the end of the academic year 1993/94, I took a sabbatical. Looking back, I think the tremendous advantage which Oslo gave us was that the Palestinian education portfolio was finally in the hands of Palestinians. We worked hard to create a better quality of education and new programmes, including a Palestinian syllabus. We believed we were not under direct military surveillance any more.

Also, Birzeit was no longer young. It was an established university that had taken on a multitude of roles in addition to its teaching one. In the absence of a national government, we had become a clinical authority, certifying locally produced medicines as well as researching and planning healthcare schemes. To ensure that our graduates did not have to emigrate, we ran an employment scheme which offered the best of them careers with us. Our staff and students provided advice and guidance services to the community.

However, the Israeli army had not gone. It was spread out all over our highways and around our towns. It even held sway over much of the countryside. The universities, it turned out, were still under military control, thanks to the checkpoints.

10

HARASSMENT AND HAIR GEL

The Israeli army has always controlled the movement of Palestinians with the help of military checkpoints, but the number of these grew exponentially after the Oslo Agreement. There are now literally hundreds of them. Some are 'flying checkpoints', set up on the hoof by soldiers who block the road with their vehicles. Others consist of a roadside hut, in which the soldiers make their tea and hold whoever they like. Yet another is a wooden tower built out of crossed planks of wood and manned by sharpshooters.

In addition, there are now sprawling, expensively built, one-storey structures designed to protect those very soldiers. Palestinians pass like cattle through narrow metal pens with a turnstile at the end – or rather wait, fenced in there, until the soldier behind the bulletproof office window can be bothered to check anyone's ID. Sometimes, a soldier suddenly leaves or moves to a window at the end of another enclosure. The queue, walking sticks, prams, shopping bags and all, has to follow the soldier there.

Palestinian IDs are passed through a thin letterbox slot in a thick door. If an ID paper raises questions, the whole queue stops. The revolving glass door just in front of the bulletproof glass window suddenly won't move and anyone in it at that point can't get out. They're stuck in a tiny, sub-divided glass case. The queue starts shouting for a soldier to move the door again, especially if the unlucky soul trapped is a child. Eventually, the soldier complies. The mood is one of humiliation and fear.

At the drive-through checkpoints towards Jerusalem, the style is cooler, but they are still designed to inspire fear. West Bankers generally can no longer get to Jerusalem, but Jerusalem Palestinians can usually move in and out in their cars – except, that is, on days when the rules change. A West Banker may tag along, hoping to pass for a Jerusalemite, or perhaps an Israeli, in the eyes of the busy soldier waving them through. Israel's problem, of course, is that unlike in South Africa, the powerful and the powerless often look alike.

However, those who want to pass need to look confident, not so easy if a breach of the rules means you end up in jail. Birzeit staff and students who have found that they live in the 'wrong' area need to take this risk every day. One lecturer said he had learned how to appear nonchalant from a book about France under occupation. Many people will risk an illegal passage only if they need to go to hospital. Others just stay home.

In any case, even legal journeys are deeply unpleasant. Waiting at checkpoints can take a very long time, as queues of waiting cars pile up.

The absurd thing is that one can fairly easily bypass the checkpoints by taking the much longer minor routes. While this is not practical for getting to work, it proves our frequently made point that the checkpoints are not really a security matter. They are just designed to make Palestinian life very difficult and so encourage emigration.

Getting to college can be impossible, as students have to pass both fixed and ever-moving Israeli checkpoints on their way there. Palestinians may not leave their own zone, but roads, towns or whole areas may also be randomly closed off. Birzeit, envisaged as a national university, now mainly caters for local students. It has lost its diversity.

Some checkpoints simply indicate the complete closure of a road. The main road leading to Birzeit goes through a small town called Surda, and this has been repeatedly closed by the army for long periods. To emphasise this point, the soldiers also dug up part of it. This means that neither cars nor buses can drive through. While this is a beautiful route from which you can see the mountains and the sea at different times, it is harsh to walk in our climate. People wanting to reach the university need to trek for an hour and a half, in the pouring rain or burning sun, to get there. One day, a group of teachers and students got so distressed they decided to hold classes on the roadside instead, sitting on the bare ground in 30° heat.

Checkpoints keep Palestinian families apart. My family is from Jerusalem, which should be 15-minutes' drive away, but the checkpoints have stopped me for over a decade from going there. Almost immediately after starting the journey you have to stop, to be asked by a young foreigner armed to the teeth what business you have going to the city. To say that you want to attend the wedding of a second cousin or the funeral of a childhood friend elucidates a contemptuous shrug, not permission to pass. Arabs are treated as habitual liars.

Our social ties are not understood. One of my professors, a man outstanding in his academic field, likes to see his parents and the rest of his family in the West Bank village of his birth every Muslim feast day. The road to the village, which used to be 50 minutes from Birzeit, is now studded with checkpoints at which travellers must halt in a queue that is often hundreds of cars long. No car may proceed until the front one is waved through. In front of the queue, groups of Israeli soldiers chat, smoke or flirt. They are not in any rush.

Sitting in a car for hours in the boiling summer heat or winter cold is uncomfortable. However, neither driver nor passengers may get out to stretch their legs or fetch a drink of water. Young children become distressed as they may not go to the toilet. If anyone opens a car door they are deemed to have lost their place in the queue. Not only does the journey regularly take five to six hours, but waiting cars are often turned back. The soldiers do not have to give any reasons. When the former British MP Oona King, who has a Jewish mother, was on an official visit to Gaza, her car with Union Jack flying was stuck at a checkpoint. Desperate to go to the lavatory, she tried to leave the car and was pushed back by a soldier. When she explained what she needed, instead of allowing her to use the checkpoint facilities the soldier told her to pee in full view under a nearby bush.

My professor friend, on the basis of his regular checkpoint experiences, claims, with just a touch of cynicism, that somewhere in one of Israel's renowned universities there is a department in which the most outstanding minds in psychology or medicine sit and deliberately work out which policies will drive us to despair, so as to encourage emigration. He may just be right.

One of the most disastrous effects of the checkpoints, in the eyes of our academic staff, has been the disruption of education. Movement restrictions play havoc with teaching schedules. The first challenge faced by every lecturer each morning is to reach the university. On leaving home, we can never know where a new checkpoint may go up, how long it will stay there or how long we will be kept waiting there.

Sometimes everybody will be delayed or sent back. At other times, only women will be allowed through, or only old people. Faced with a group of students, a soldier may decide to let only the tall ones through, or only short ones.

On reaching the university, a professor may find that there is no way of getting an exam printed, a paper copied or a book ordered that day due to the absence of administrative staff. Attending an academic conference or doing one's research may be impossible because of travel restrictions. There may also be no one to teach. When a certain highway or village is blocked off, a third of one's class may be absent. Having a full class, with all the students on the register actually present, is becoming a rare occasion.

One of our professors found himself teaching a class of one student not long ago. The lucky student explained that at his checkpoint, the officer in charge had decided that only boys wearing hair gel would get through. 'Today, I decide,' the soldier told the waiting group, 'and I say that hair gel is today's ticket to Birzeit.'

The academic often has to customise a lesson for an individual student, because he or she may have missed out as a result of such incidents. Other students disappear because they have been arrested, either at home or at a checkpoint. When they re-emerge three or four weeks later, they need to catch up, but cannot concentrate. It is hard to inculcate study habits or attitudes of mind if there is sporadic attendance. Students miss exams and sometimes have to repeat a year.

A report issued in January 2009 put the number of Birzeit students incarcerated since November 2003 at 372. Of these, 84 were still in jail 14 months later, 40 of them without charge. One Birzeit student has been held in administrative detention for three years.

To keep up standards in such circumstances is a constant challenge. A lecturer sometimes has to be prepared to fail a student or to give him/her a low grade, while knowing that this student has been in jail or been traumatised in some other way. Students have been known to arrive at university with half-healed fractures or bullet wounds. Others have seen a friend or relative injured. Asked by a passing journalist if the occupation had affected him, one of our students revealed that his brother had been shot in the thigh, his brother-in-law had lost an eye and a distant cousin had been killed.

The most painful thing to cope with for staff, of course, was the killing of a student. The number of university students killed from 1976 to 2007 is a staggering 199, and that does not include the Israeli assault on Gaza in December 2008 and January 2009. However well you are prepared for bad news, such a death is still deeply shocking. Staff become distressed and find it hard to work. People ferrying the wounded are often stopped by soldiers from driving on to a hospital. One young man, shot by the army, bled to death in a lecturer's car.

Talking in 2008, one of our professors described the effects which the announcement of a student's deaths would have on her:

> I would go back to my office, and look at my computer with a gut feeling of nausea, sadness and grief. But one had to try and act as if life went on as normal. Retaining one's focus was painfully hard, an endless struggle. But it was also a challenge to us, our kind of people, to withstand all this pressure and still continue to work at the highest possible level. Birzeit had to remain academically credible, we had to keep up professionalism and quality.

Events that happened at home may also cause an academic to arrive at work in a state of distress. Maths professor Marwan Awartani recalls that during the first intifada, his five-year-old son was flying kites made of multi-coloured paper outside their home. The family lived only a few hundred yards from the army's West Bank headquarters and one of the sentries mistook the child's kite for a Palestinian flag. 'As a result,' the father recalls:

> two military jeeps screeched to a stop outside our house. A soldier got out, grabbed my son and put him on the jeep. What the kid was holding was a kite, not a flag. These kids were just having fun, it was not a conspiracy or an attempt to invade Israel. My wife started to cry and beg. We ran after the jeep and, after the longest 20 minutes of my life, the soldiers let the child go. As he ran off, an officer turned to me and warned me that he would hold us accountable if the same thing ever happened again.

As the army still controls our access roads, the parents among our staff members still become very anxious at times. A boy who does not arrive at home may have been detained, or a parent may be unable to collect a girl from school because the road there has been closed.

One student described the first time he was arrested:

> Most first-year students at Birzeit get arrested at some point by the occupation forces, so they can get information about us, particularly about the way we think, so they can keep tabs on us whilst we're at university. In my first year, the army

came and took people randomly every week. When they came for me, the soldier who put the handcuffs on me started talking to me. He was whispering, so the captain didn't hear him. 'How do you live like this? How do you handle it?' he asked. 'We manage,' I told him. 'That's all we can do. And it's not like you – you have many options we don't have. All we have now is education, so I study.' He told me that at his university he had problems paying the tuition, and how did I find the money for it? I told him, 'It's hard, but it's all I have, so I find a way, somehow.' But in the end, he was a soldier, and he tied me up and took me away.

One of Israel's key projects has always been to detach the Gaza Strip's population from their fellow Palestinians in Jerusalem and the West Bank. Just before the re-opening of Birzeit in 1991, the military government had tried to stop Gaza students from coming to the university. When I met with Gadi Zohar, the new commander of the West Bank at the time, he asked me: 'What do you want with the Gaza students? They only give you trouble!'

Zohar's line was based on Israel's old divide-and-rule policy. I had not forgotten the time when the military governor had asked us: 'Why do you need all these foreign faculty members coming to teach? You can do without them.' Pretending to have our interests at heart, the Israelis were really trying to persuade us to do what was good for them.

I made it clear that Birzeit had an open door policy for all Palestinian students and that we would continue to have students from all over the West Bank and Gaza. We would not reject anyone on the basis of their geographic location. After noting our strong position on this, the commander started bargaining by saying that he would let the current group of Gaza students complete their studies, but we would not be allowed to admit new ones. I replied that it was up to the students to choose which university they wanted to attend. Besides, the two universities in Gaza did not offer all the courses students wanted, such as engineering.

Zohar would not give up, saying: 'We can open a school of engineering for them in Gaza.' I asked in reply: 'Since when do you start university programmes and determine what universities Palestinians should have and where?'

I brought up the example of Israel: 'It is unthinkable to tell a student from Haifa that he should go to Haifa University and that he should not go to Hebrew University in Jerusalem, simply because he is from Haifa.' I then added: 'We must have the same rights as Israeli students, including the right to attend the universities of their choice.'

Alas, Zohar did not relent. The Israelis had made up their mind to isolate Gaza as much as possible and prevent its students from coming here. It is not that they actually wanted them to study nearer home, of course. A few years later, in the winter of 2008–09, they would bomb Gaza's university.

What the Israelis believed was that the Gaza students had been more active during the intifada than the West Bank ones. In fact, I think that they were, if anything, less active because most young people from Gaza were studying science or engineering, tough courses that are highly competitive. Birzeit was far from their home, forcing them to pass a large number of checkpoints. Many also had to hide the fact that they were staying in Birzeit 'illegally', that is, without a residence permit. So Gaza students who wanted to come to Birzeit tended to be highly motivated and did very well in their studies. They could not have done so without investing a lot of time in their academic work.

While some Gaza students are indeed inclined towards the Islamist movement, the proportion among them is not much higher than among others. Certainly, the Israeli claim that we were picking Gaza students because they were political could not have been further from the truth. We are a high-quality institution and students are selected on a competitive basis. Only the best are admitted and if they want to stay at the university, they have to work hard. Students are encouraged to participate in extracurricular activities because that is part of the university message. However, that of course did not mean violent activities. What students were encouraged to do was to play a role in the community of Birzeit.

From the start, Birzeit students have been part of their respective communities. They were generally quite aware of what is going on around them and they were vocal in expressing their rights. They had their own views on how things should be. None of them would tolerate occupation and oppression. They knew their rights and they knew what they were doing. Perhaps this is why Birzeit and its students were victimised more than students at other institutions. Birzeit was a leader and the Israelis felt that by punishing the leaders they would send a message to other universities and students.

A report about Gaza published during the 1990s revealed that, in proportional terms, there were fewer Gazans than West Bankers in Israeli prisons. This disproves the image painted by the Israelis to the outside world about the 'evil' Gaza students.

Over time, the Israelis used other methods, such as Order 854, to keep out the Gazans. However, we never agreed to apply for permits from the military governor for them. Whatever methods the Israelis used, we would not give in. It was the post-Oslo movement restrictions which finally made it almost impossible for Gazans to study with us. However, we remain keen to preserve the diversity of Birzeit's Palestinian student body and a few are still there.

While we are not yet free, we have always been able to teach our students about the key element in freedom, which is democracy. Asked to make an entry in the annual issue of the university year-book one day, I wrote: 'Democracy is not something you learn in books; it is something you have to practise and if we are going to have democracy we have to practise it first in our universities.'

Democratic values were something that we tried to inculcate in students through university practices from the start. In a society in which the concept is not practised anywhere, this is quite a challenge. Children certainly do not observe democracy in their homes, nor is it practised in schools. Birzeit, even as a high school and a junior college, granted a considerable amount of freedom of expression to students to practise those ideals in direct debates, or in student papers or on bulletin boards. We owe a good deal of this to our academic staff, who by and large set a good example to the students. We owe much to the students as well, who spoke up and suggested improvements which we implemented.

We started student organisation activities early in the 1960s when Birzeit was still a junior college and students joined various clubs for extra-curricular activities. The heads of these clubs consti-tuted the Student Council. Although they were elected by the club members, this system meant that they were not elected by all the students. Later, we appointed a staff member as head of student affairs, and he would eventually work out a set of rules for the student elections and the student council.

In the early 1970s, when we moved from our two-year to our four-year programme, student elections were becoming more organised and were recognised as important by the students. The Israeli occupation politicised the student body. Election campaigns became more sophisticated, so that students running for election could debate their platform in a spot they called 'Hyde Park Corner' after Speaker's Corner in London's Hyde Park, where anyone can stand up and make a speech. Electioneering stopped

The author with Dr Hanan Ashrawi during a reception for the first Palestinian Legislative Council, 1996

one day before election day, which meant that all posters and other campaign signs had to be removed from campus. Voting ended at 5 pm. The students and the Dean of Students would then stay up until midnight to count the votes in front of the student representatives.

Students awaited the outcome with bated breath, but both the local and foreign press also took an interest in the result. This was because the Birzeit student body included students from all over the occupied territories, from Gaza in the south to Tulkarm and Jenin in the north. We had students from rural areas and from cities. Women and men represented students from all social groups. All had been selected on the basis of their high-school matriculation grades. Financial status did not matter, as suitable applicants could gain an exemption from fees. So our students were representative demographically as well as politically. The ratios of the winning groups to one another reflected the political mood within the whole of Palestinian society in the occupied territories.

From the early 1980s onwards, the student factions included the Islamic Bloc, which did not recognise the PLO. This introduced a new element of 'excitement' – to say the least – into the elections. In 1992, after the first intifada, when teaching was again permitted

The author with Dr Haidar Abdul Shafi, 1996

on campus, we held Student Council elections. For the first time ever, votes were counted electronically (followed by hand counting as a double check). This election, the one observed by the PEACE Programme, served as a precursor to the democratic elections we would eventually hold in Palestine.

The first Palestinian elections, held in 1996, were indeed a bright spot. For the first time we were able to elect a President and a Legislative Council. It was a slightly odd situation. Encouraging people to elect a president implied that in fact we had a state, but we believed we did. In our search for peace, we tried to overlook the fact that Israel was still imposing hurdles and restrictions on movement, building settlements and expropriating land. We continued to act as if things were proceeding normally.

To do so, I think, was our biggest mistake. Soon people became angry about the way in which the Palestinian National Authority (a government without a state) was handling things. It suddenly looked as if the negotiations we were involved in were not roads to a solution but an end in itself. We seemed to have lost our dignity and self-respect. In our relations with Israel, we had to compromise all the time and Israel did not stop putting pressure on the Palestinians for one moment.

International solidarity groups became less willing to help the Palestinians. They thought that the Oslo Accords had finally brought about peace. This was a major fallacy. Having peace negotiations was not the same as having peace, as advocacy groups tried to point out. The Palestinian Council for Justice and Peace, established in 1996, sought to explain what was really happening to solidarity groups from all over the world.

What we had gained from the negotiations with Israel was the right to run our own ministries. The portfolio for education was the first to be handed over to the Palestinians, in September 1994. It gave the responsibility for all Arab education in the occupied territories, except East Jerusalem, to the Palestinian National Authority (PNA).

Jerusalem was different for historical reasons. There were public schools that had been taken over completely by the Israeli government. Others had been unofficially under the auspices of the Jordanian government. Later on, these were transferred to the Islamic Waqf (Islamic Foundation) in Jordan. Then there were private schools which had implemented the Jordanian curriculum before Oslo, and later the Palestinian syllabus.

Since the Oslo agreements and the handover of responsibility for education to the PNA, there have been few closures of universities or colleges, although we saw some school closures for 'security reasons'. In the wake of the 1994 Hebron massacre committed at the Ibrahimi Mosque by Baruch Goldstein, a religious Israeli from Brooklyn, strict curfews shut down all the educational institutions in that region. Al-Quds University and Hebron University were both closed in 1994 by the Israeli authorities, as both were still in the area under Israeli control.

The Council for Higher Education was still functioning, and continued to be responsible for the university sector until June 1996. It remained autonomous, reporting directly to the Palestinian Ministry of Education and Higher Education.

There were around ten departments in this ministry. These covered technical education, community colleges, buildings and grounds, examinations, orientation and supervision of school curricula, cultural activities, public relations and so on. It was run fairly well, although it was understaffed and suffered from terrible financial problems. The ministry was supported by the general funding that was coming to the Palestinians from the European Community, the World Bank and other bodies.

The offices of the Ministry of Education and Higher Education were dispersed, which was awkward. The main ones were in Ramallah in the West Bank, although they were supposed to be in Gaza and Jericho when the Palestinian Authority was first established. There were offices in these two cities but the Ramallah office was the main one, euphemistically called a 'department', because we were not supposed to have a ministry in Ramallah.

The work of the ministry was enormous. For 27 years, education had suffered from criminal neglect under the Israelis. The ministry sought to improve the quality of education. It tried to recruit good teachers, since many of the current ones were not qualified, but this was expensive and in any case you could not simply kick people out and replace them. So we set up in-service training instead, another big job.

As for the school buildings and infrastructure, these were in poor shape and insufficient for our needs. We needed more and better schools, equipment, simple furniture, elementary laboratory facilities and so on in order to cope with the growing number of students.

The curriculum, too, needed to be updated, because it had been left largely untouched by the Israelis. Teachers were still using Jordanian and Egyptian syllabuses from 1967. In a burst of wishful thinking, the Israelis had merely removed the words 'Palestine' or 'Palestinian' from all texts and replaced them with the words 'Israel' or 'Israeli'. Its officials had also deleted all references to the Palestinian–Israeli conflict and its national implications, including the geography of Palestine.

Curriculum content also needed to be standardised, as Gaza was following the Egyptian syllabus while the West Bank used the Jordanian one. This was a major undertaking, especially as we were preparing a national syllabus while having neither full statehood nor peace with our occupiers. Teaching geography, for instance, could mean having to teach borders which were still unknown. We resorted to teaching 'Palestine under the mandate', and referred to all towns and villages as parts of historic Palestine. The Israelis objected that this meant we did not recognise Israel. Our argument was that, until Israel decided where its borders were, we would continue to use historic Palestine as our base.

What still had to be negotiated with the Israelis was the so-called 'security' issue. They still had the authority to close schools and sometimes did. As far as they were concerned, anyone throwing stones from a school was threatening the security of Israel. When students demonstrated on the streets in the occupied territories outside Gaza and Jericho, the army also still got involved.

Problems of resources would arise time and time again. This was a worry for us, especially in relation to teachers' salaries. We still did not have our own tax system or resources, so the EU and the World Bank continued to be our major donors. Their aid was not tied. They simply wanted to see that it was spent on specific projects and was audited properly.

In the ministry, we were working with UNESCO on school mapping, finding out the educational needs in each school in the West Bank and Gaza Strip. UNESCO was also helping with curriculum development and sending some experts to help. They were creating lists of needs and arranging them into projects that could be funded by donor countries. UNRWA continued to maintain its own schools, which now came under the umbrella of the Ministry of Education (in the same fashion that they related to the Israeli education system prior to 1994). UNRWA schools still maintained their autonomous structure, and their relationship with the Ministry of Education and Higher Education was similar to that in other Arab countries.

The advent of the Palestinian Authority, sadly, caused a polarisation in Palestinian society. The conflict between those who supported it and those who did not deflected attention from issues relating to the occupation. The Israeli army was no longer constantly visible. People would only become aware of it again during closures, at the checkpoints, or when its soldiers assassinated Palestinian faction members.

The Israeli policy of collective punishment was continued. Al-Quds and Hebron Universities were closed for several months by military order. Surda checkpoint between Ramallah and Birzeit could still turn the ten-minute trip to the university into an agonizing one or two-hour marathon for students and staff. There was no protest from the Israeli universities against any of these actions against the Palestinian universities, which were making the daily lives of the university community unbearable. Our Israeli colleagues ignored our problems, although there were constant appeals by Birzeit against its treatment.

The political situation affected the university as well. While in the past students had been united against the Israeli occupation, we now had students who supported the Palestinian National Authority and students who supported the opposition. At the same time, we had to confront the bad behaviour of the Authority, with its poor administration and corruption.

Disappointment steadily grew and was reflected in Student Council elections. Many Birzeit graduates who supported the PLO,

including some Fateh members, started feeling that their leadership was unaware of what was happening on the ground. Some
grumbled that better leaders would not have allowed the Israelis to
leave the issue of the Israeli settlements until later (if they were ever
to deal with it at all).

The state of euphoria certainly did not last long. Rabin was
dragging his feet in implementing even the already agreed territorial
withdrawals. Even more dangerous was the fact that he was talking
about peace while going ahead with the building of settlements that
would preserve Israeli hegemony in the occupied territories. Rabin's
assassination by a religious Israel student did not help. Subsequent governments continued his policy of land expropriation and
settlement construction.

Palestinians felt betrayed and were furious. Their accumulated
anger led to the eruption of the second intifada after Ariel Sharon's
provocative visit to the Al-Aqsa mosque in the year 2000. Led by
uncompromising Islamists, it was vastly more violent and unselec-
tive in its targets than the first intifada had been. What prompted
this uprising was the Palestinian realisation that Israel had no
serious intentions of making peace. It was not willing to give up,
or change, its longstanding commitment to a Jewish state in all of
Palestine, or at best in most of it.

This, of course, was no basis for peace. Peace requires justice
and the observance of international laws. In our case, this meant
especially the laws that enshrine the right of return for Palestinian
refugees and the self-determination for Palestinians on their own
land. Israel was talking peace but on the ground it was waging war.
Even after the Oslo Accords, the building of settlements continued
and even accelerated.

Taken together with the destruction of our homes, the expropriation of our land and the creation of hundreds of checkpoints
(which I prefer to call 'choke points') this gives the lie to Israel's
avowals of a desire for peace. Israel's construction of the apartheid
Wall which breaks up Palestinian territory into small, powerless and
disconnected cantons is another indication of its real intent.

All this suggests that the future for Palestinians is bleak, but we
are a steadfast people and have already shown that we can resist
Israel's repressive policies in a huge number of ways. Nor must we
always fight violence with violence. One alternative path towards
regaining our rights is strong pressure from abroad.

I therefore welcomed the launch of the 2004 Palestinian Academic
and Cultural Boycott of Israel (PACBI) campaign. This has created a

new way for international groups and individuals to make a statement of their distaste for Israel's policies by breaking organisational links with Israeli institutions and linking up with ours instead. PACBI is gaining momentum and has already received support from 170 local academic and cultural bodies and unions.

Joining PACBI is an act of resistance to the occupation. Through the campaign, the international community can exert pressure on Israel to stop its violations of human rights and to abandon its policies aimed at making life unbearable for Palestinians. PACBI might enable the rest of the world to join us in derailing Israel's hidden plan to ethnically cleanse Palestine of its indigenous Moslem and Christian Arab population.

11

PREACHING TO THE CHOIR

The last ten years have been marked by increasing media coverage given to the nature of Israel's oppression of the Palestinians, and we have to be grateful for that. Such attention may not change governments, but it certainly makes Palestinians feel less alone in their plight. Paradoxically, however, it can create the impression that we must all be wandering round depressed, deprived and disheartened. Certainly, as the events in Gaza in 2008/9 showed, Palestinians have been subject to horrific and illegal abuses by Israel, and many have died, been maimed for life, or bereaved. But under the stress of our situation, we just have to try to carry on and live an everyday life that people in other societies take for granted.

Music is one of the things which helped me cope with the occupation. I was one of the founding members of the community choir known as the Jerusalem Chorus, back in 1955. The Chorus brings together local people, university staff, students and residents from the international community, all with a love for music. Every Tuesday for several decades the university's minibus would take us to Jerusalem for choir practice.

Our main focus has always been classical music. Our repertoire includes Mozart's *Coronation Mass*, Beethoven's oratorio *Christ on the Mount of Olives*, Haydn's *Mass in Time of War*, Haydn's *Creation*, Schubert's *Mass in C*, Faure's *Requiem*, Brahms' *German Requiem*, Vivaldi's *Gloria*, choral pieces from Bach oratorios and Handel's *Messiah*. However, we also sing Christmas carols in winter, as well as lighter works and choral pieces from famous operas in our spring concert. We have recently added some Arabic songs composed by local composers for special occasions.

Choir practice took place in the Jerusalem YWCA and I never missed a rehearsal, even during the most difficult days. Singing gave me some energy for the rest of the week. The choir was a friendly group of around 40 people and it made a change from the harsh reality of living under a military government.

But a benign activity like my membership of a choir puzzled the Israelis. One Monday, I was summoned to the military governor's office late in the night. Ariel Sharon was Defence Minister then, and on the way to the Muqata'a I complained about Israel's policies and the closure of our university to the officer who was accompanying me to the governor's office. I said I wanted to see the Minister of Defence, to which the officer's reply was 'Sharon is not Weizman.'

When we finally reached the Muqata'a, I was put into a room next to the governor's office. The officer there seemed apologetic and asked me to make myself comfortable and to wait. I was curious, as this was not the usual waiting room. Finally it clicked and I asked whether I was being arrested. The officer did not reply, which meant yes. I asked him to send news to my family about my arrest. I also needed the container for my contact lenses and my toothbrush.

I then settled down on the sofa to wait, while working my way through a fruit bowl on the table. I could not sleep and kept hearing the telephone ring at the governor's office. There were numerous calls and he was asking his aides to say he had gone out. I wanted to believe that the calls were from people in solidarity with Birzeit who were pressing the governor to release me.

The author giving a speech during the official medal ceremony at the French Consulate General in Jerusalem, 1993

I was not completely wrong. After two hours, Major Shmulik, the new military governor of Ramallah, told me that they had an order to arrest me. However, I was being given special treatment by being asked to wait in the governor's room instead of in jail. He then informed me that I was under town arrest, which meant that I was not allowed to leave Ramallah.

This was bad news given my musical plans for the next day and I pointed out that I had to go to Jerusalem on Tuesday evenings. The Major asked why. I explained that I had choir practice. At this, he was dumbfounded and did not know whether I was serious or not. Nothing more was said by him and I did not comment further. I then called Haifa and asked her to come and pick me up. That Tuesday I went to Jerusalem for my choir practice as usual. I was never stopped or questioned.

After my release, Haifa told me what happened. When she heard that I was under arrest, she immediately went to see Hanan Ashrawi, who was heading the Birzeit committee liaising with lawyers who aided people arrested for political reasons. Hanan called our lawyer, Lea Tsemel. My wife waited with Hanan for some time at the Muqata'a, wondering what would happen. The officer asked them to leave, saying that I would not be released that night. They persisted however, and luckily I got out.

Sometimes events inspired our choice of music. In 2002 we sang Haydn's *Mass in Time of War* in the Church of Beit Jala which was hit by Israeli tanks during the huge incursion into the West Bank cities at that time, and called the programme 'Music against Bombardment'.

A few years later, when the Wall went up and soldiers prevented us from entering Jerusalem at the Kalandia checkpoint, we got out of our bus and stood there singing Christmas carols and Arabic patriotic songs. One of the effects of the Wall has been that the Jerusalem choir can no longer enter Jerusalem.

It is a wonderful choir. At first, its members were only Christians, but then they were joined by Muslims who liked to sing, and by international residents. The choir's conductor, Salwa Tabri, was so committed to the choir that she continued in her task even from a wheelchair when she developed multiple sclerosis. She would say that the choir kept her alive. Until 1995, we would arrange exchange visits with choirs abroad.

Being members of the choir has enriched our lives. Once, the Choir of London agreed to an exchange visit with us. We were far less professional than they were, but the members of our choir were inspired to do their very best. The music raised our spirits as well as

The author receiving a medal (the Palme Academique) from the Consul General, during the official medal ceremony at the French Consulate General in Jerusalem, 1993

erasing the borders hemming us in from all sides. Rita Giacaman, a Birzeit public health professor, described the collaboration with the Choir of London as one of the most uplifting in her life: 'We were only amateurs, not full-time singers like some of our visitors. Still, we really flew that night,' she said. 'Afterwards, none of us could sleep.'

Israel's military occupation of Palestinian land has the wide support of many Israelis, as well as a proportion of Jews overseas. But in our regular confrontations with the ceaseless onslaught of the occupation regime against the Palestinian people we have been supported by a handful of Jews, including some Israelis. In spite of what supporters of Israel say, being critical of Israel is not anti-Semitic, since there are Jews who are as appalled as we are at what is done in the name of the Jewish state.

I have met and come to respect the small number of politicised Israelis who want their country to take the route of justice and humanity and are actively committed to achieving this. The rights of Birzeit University have been defended and actively supported by a handful of Israeli lawyers, journalists and academics. But our opposition is not just to the deeds perpetrated against us by the Israelis, but to the false ideas they propagate.

Let me illustrate this. At the entrance to Ben Gurion airport is a huge sign displaying a saying by the founder of political Zionism, Theodor Herzl: 'If you want it, it is not a fairy tale.'

Unfortunately, however much Israelis 'want' a Palestine without the Palestinians, we are still here. We have been here since time immemorial. Our homes, churches, mosques, trees and family memories bear witness to this fact. In the case of Palestine, wanting it to be free of Palestinian Arabs is a fairy tale.

The history of the airport itself, where this empty phrase of Herzl's is displayed, reflects Israel's attempts to destroy the Palestinians. It is built on the land of Arab villages. Refugees from one of those, Beit Nabalah, now live in Jalazon refugee camp. Israel needs to acknowledge that we, too, are a nation, which means we want to educate ourselves, enable our people to get on in life and end the misery of our refugees. Unless Israeli governments acknowledge this, it will be impossible to contain the violence. Our desire – recognition of our age-long connection with the land – is no fairy tale.

In order to resolve the conflict, some of us have tried to learn more about Jews and about Israelis. Many of us know about the holocaust; we can grasp its effects even on those Jews who did not actually suffer it, in the fear that some of them feel about a recurrence in the future. But the Israeli determination to dispossess us is not a way of combating fear, merely a form of colonial thinking. Nothing that happened in the holocaust justifies our *Nakba*. For a start, the Nazis were Germans, Europeans – not Palestinians. We are the indigenous population of this Middle Eastern country.

Also, the holocaust has acquired a uniqueness of suffering in Jewish eyes, which seems to blind them to the suffering they cause themselves. We can sympathize with them, but Israelis seem to lack all empathy with us. As far as they are concerned, suffering only counts if it meets certain quantitative standards. If six million Palestinians have not been killed, we have nothing to complain about. There seems to be no awareness that every tortured individual, every parent who loses a child, every child deprived of a parent, suffers in exactly the same way.

Blinded by their narrow perspective, to judge by the governments they elect, most Israeli Jews lack all sense of universal human rights. They cannot see us as human beings, cannot believe that people will never accept certain ways of being treated, that human rights apply everywhere, and that means here too.

At the same time, the international community has been inhibited in the past from criticising Israeli policies by its politicians' constant references to the holocaust. Despite the shocking reports that come out of the occupied territories, people abroad still find it hard to grasp that it is possible for a group to be victims in one generation and perpetrators of crimes in the next. The Yugoslav Serbs, who suffered greatly under the Nazis yet imposed a murderous regime on the Bosnian people 50 years later, are another example.

We spent years hearing Israelis complain that we would not recognise them, even though it seemed strange that we should, given what they had done to us. Still, there is now formal recognition. The Madrid talks, in which Birzeit played a key role, were an expression of this. But now it is time that Israelis recognise us as people of equal rights. How can Jews, the world's most education-oriented people, seek to destroy our children's prospects of learning?

What has enabled Birzeit to survive is our determination to stay calm in the face of provocation. This did not mean that we never got angry. The important thing was to control the feeling, so as to react with equanimity to the constant direct and indirect attacks on Palestinian education. We were determined not to give in and not to appear cowed by the Israelis.

On the one hand, Birzeit was a normal university with factional politics and academic differences that had to be reconciled somehow. Talented academic staff, if they were to stay, needed to feel at home. On the other hand, running the university meant one had to be ready for the unpredictable, for raids, sieges, checkpoint troubles, and deadly attacks on students.

It was important to create an atmosphere in which academics felt inspired to do more than just carry out their basic duties. Given the state of our homeland, they needed to develop our students, and instil in them good learning habits and attitudes of mind. We, the university leaders, cared about students' lives, but also needed to show the kind of firmness that ensured they met our academic standards. The administrative process too had to run smoothly. The university had to be a place in which good people could flourish; it had to encourage the quest for knowledge, not just its absorption.

What mattered no less was to retain one's vision for the future, that of a Palestinian university that would be democratic and liberal, as well as providing a patriotic open space for students and the wider community. We were determined to keep an academically credible institution going, despite all outside pressure.

Among the students, we looked for people with the Birzeit spirit. This meant they were selfless, group spirited and community

A Jerusalem Chorus concert at the YWCA Jerusalem, 1980

oriented, capable of feeling solidarity with others. The motto we picked for Birzeit was: 'Seek happiness in doing a job well.'

We were trying to create leaders of their communities, well-rounded individuals prepared to build a successful new society and move towards a free Palestine. Our graduates continue to stand out in their communities. We have educated many of Palestine's political leaders, including Ghassan Khatib, the Minister of Planning, Bassam Salhi, a member of the Legislative Council and head of the People's Party, Marwan Barghouti, the jailed political leader of Fateh, Mohammad Shtayyeh of PECDAR, Hassan Abu Libdeh, the Minister of Social Affairs and later head of the Palestine Monetary Fund.

In the international academic field, we have brought forth a high number of outstanding professors. Gabriel Alexander Khoury of Imperial College London is also a professor for life at Padua University, Italy. Mujid Kazimi is at the Massachusetts Institute of Technology (MIT), Salim Tamari is at Birzeit University and Khalil Mahshi at UNESCO/IIE in Paris, to name a few.

We also learned to live with different agendas being pursued at the university. As one of our student committee leaders once somewhat flippantly put it to me: 'It's a division of labour. We students keep the national flag flying as high as possible, while the university administration keeps the academic level as high as possible.' In reality, of course, running a university under occupation required far more than that. Birzeit had to be a place in which people could develop the skills they would need one day for a free, democratic society.

As students started to disappear into jail, we also became the first port of call for prisoners' families, and our legal aid liaison office set up a prisoners' committee consisting of academic staff, students and internationals. The committee's first job was always to find out the names of everyone arrested and their ID numbers. With those details, our lawyers could apply for an order nisi (a legal term meaning to stop the specific action). Without an order nisi, those picked up were in danger of being expelled to Lebanon or jailed. Students were sometimes put under house arrest or town arrest for an unlimited period, so they could not return to their studies.

Still, we looked out for everyone. Students who were arrested had their university places kept for them. Even if they were in jail for a year or more, we would let them come back and help them to catch up. Those exiled to Jordan or Lebanon during their course were sent examination papers.

We at Birzeit acted *in loco parentis*, and in place of a government. The problem is that our students do generally have parents, and they now even have a 'government'. What our students don't have is a state, and that means they possess no power over their

The author with US President Jimmy Carter at the US Consulate General in Jerusalem, 1993

lives. They are not free people. Their cities, towns, villages, schools and universities are surrounded by Israel's tanks, jeeps, army bases and settlements. They are persecuted and frequently killed by Israeli soldiers. This makes them a symbol of the Palestinian fate.

This book has been an attempt to make the existence and the merits of our generations of students more widely known. In the face of daily Israeli insults and assaults on your identity or even your right to live, it is easy to become despondent and discouraged. That we don't is perhaps due to the characteristic described by the Arabic word *sumud*, which I believe Palestinians have in abundance. The word means 'steadfastness', and no one observing the daily pursuit of teaching and learning at Birzeit University can be unaware of its value in the face of attempts to disrupt the educational process.

The individual stories in this book are not told to draw attention to the cleverness of any individual at outwitting an occupation which is, in any case, witless (a bull in a china shop cannot really take credit for the skill with which it destroys crockery). Israel has sometimes laughably described itself as a David in the face of an Arab Goliath, but if there are Davids facing Goliath in the illegal occupation it is the administrators who refused to be cowed by uniformed people with stars on their epaulettes or Birzeit students with their stones daring to confront the IDF.

Taking a holistic view of my life's work at Birzeit and in Palestinian education, I believe it has taught me that there is an effective role for peaceful resistance under impossible conditions and against all odds, where both extreme physical and psychological means are used against the people to crush their will to resist and even exist, and to prevail upon them to leave their homes and country. Our success in peaceful resistance was achieved through considerable pain and humiliation. It required qualities such as perseverance, dignity, strength of character, using our wits (necessity is the mother of invention) and above all a strong belief in our cause along with the knowledge that we are right.

Palestine is our homeland; its fields, fruits, landscapes, villages, holy sites, archaeology, hills and coastline have been an integral part of our life and the lives of our ancestors for generations past. Many of us still keep safe the deeds to our stolen properties and the keys of our stolen houses, but in all of us Palestine will always remain in our hearts and collective memory, and it is where ultimately we will return. Along with photographs, traditional dress and stories passed down the generations, they constitute powerful symbols of legal ownership of the land stolen from us. The saying goes that right is might, even if we are in a hopelessly weak military position.

Birzeit was founded by Palestinians who are peaceful. The founder of Birzeit College, Musa Nasir, set the tone of positive non-violent action to serve the community within the spirit of Birzeit – that of placing the public good above one's own interest. I was brought up in this spirit and lived all my active life practising what I believed in. Education is at the heart of any nation and helps equip young people with the knowledge and culture that provides an extra layer of strength and the capability necessary to cope with a harsh and unrelenting occupation. Our resistance was peaceful in nature and we did our best to educate our students and instil in them the culture of true democracy to prepare them to live in a free, peaceful and democratic society – in a state of their own.

We succeeded to a large degree not only in stopping the brain drain from Palestine but actually reversing it. By developing the university – the concept as well as the physical structure – we created an obstacle in the path of the ethnic cleansing of Palestine which has been the hallmark of the powerful Zionist state from its inception 60 years ago. Fortunately, the majority of the nations of this world understand the plight of the Palestinians and the justice of their cause. There is also hope now that the US government will realise the truth and stand up to Israeli violations of human rights.

This book forms part of the peaceful resistance process. It records for posterity the achievements and successes of peaceful resistance in the face of unrelenting oppression. We believe that the pen is mightier than the sword. This book is aimed at people in the West, and among the Jewish communities, who have been unwittingly supporting Zionist ethnic cleansing and oppression in Palestine, believing Zionist lies and half-truths. We hope that the facts presented in this book will provide those people with the Pauline experience of seeing the light in order to help end their unwitting persecution of a whole nation, albeit indirectly, through their support for Zionism.

We believe that the lessons to be learnt from our actions can be helpful anywhere in the world where occupied people face oppression, and we hope that the story is worth telling, if only to bring the world's attention to how a peaceful non-violent resistance can be effective, and to raise support and sympathy to help the generations of students who will form the core administration of the future state of Palestine.

APPENDIX I

CHRONOLOGY OF BIRZEIT UNIVERSITY

1924	Birzeit Higher School established by Miss Nabiha Nasir.
1942	Name 'Birzeit College' adopted.
1951	Musa Nasir becomes principal of the college after his sister Nabiha passes away.
1953	University-level freshman classes in arts and science started.
1961	University-level sophomore classes added.
1962	Associate status in arts and science degrees granted.
1962	Primary and secondary sections phased out gradually, and in 1967 the college programme was limited to the freshman and sophomore classes.
1971	Hanna Nasir becomes president after his father passes away.
1972	Start of development of four-year programme leading to bachelors' degrees in arts and in sciences.
1973	Founders form an autonomous board of trustees that assumes full responsibility for the institution.
1974	Addition of academic junior year.
1974	Hanna Nasir is deported and vice president Gabi Baramki assumes responsibility for the administration of the university.
1975	Addition of academic senior year.
1975	Official name change to Birzeit University.
1976	Joins the Association of Arab Universities.
1977	Joins International Association of Universities.
1978	Adds Faculty of Commerce and Economics.
1979	Adds Faculty of Engineering.
1988	Military order closes the university in January until April 1992.
1993	Hanna Nasir returns and resumes his duties as president and Gabi Baramki retires after 40 years in service of the institution.

2004   Nabeel Kassis becomes president after Hanna Nasir retires.

1993–2009 Several new faculties and centres are established, including law and public administration, women's studies, media and graduate studies.

APPENDIX II

DEPORTATION STATEMENT OF HANNA NASIR, NOVEMBER 1974

Memorandum by
Dr. Hanna Musa Nasir
President of Birzeit College
On His Deportation from the West Bank of Jordan

On the 21st of November 1974, the Israeli
military government deported me along with four
other members** from the Israeli Occupied West
Bank of Ordan to Lebanon. The alleged reason
was simply stated as "security violations" and
was indicated when a deportation order was read
to us at the border with Lebanon. Incidentally,
the order made reference to a 1945 British
mandate regulation.

The deportation came in the wake of the
recent demonstrations that spread over
most of the West Bank. The demonstrations
expressed solidarity with the Palestinian
Liberation organization and coincided with the
demonstrations about Palestine going on in the
U.N. The demonstrations were basically limited
to students, but were spread amongst most
schools. There was also a strike by shopkeepers

---

* Dr. Alfred Toubassi – Dentist and Member of Ramallah
  Municipal Council Mr. Abdel Razzak Audeh – Contrac-
  tor and Member of Ramallah Chamber of Commerce. Mr.
  Mahmoud Quadry – High School Teacher. Mr. Ghattas
  Abu Ayteh – High School Teacher.

in Ramallah on Wednesday morning. The strike
lasted till noon when most shops were forced to
open by the Israeli army.

   According to a Military Government's
statement which was published in the Jerusalem
Post, the reasons for my departure were given
as incitement of the students of Birzeit and
Ramallah to demonstrate and incitement which
lead to the shop-keepers' strike in Ramallah.

   I categorically and emphatically deny and
refute all the alleged charges. It is true that
the students of Birzeit College demonstrated.
It would have been futile to even attempt and
stop the demonstrations and my role was to
control things as much as possible and avert
a confrontation with the army. I had heard
earlier about clashes between school-children
and the army in which one student was killed
and several were injured and I was worried that
similar things might happen in Birzeit.
Luckily, I was successful in averting a
confrontation. Mr. Terence Smith – a New York
Times correspondent – witnessed my actions and
reported that in the November 22nd issue of the
N.Y.T. Later on in that day, a couple of our
students were arrested (for carrying
Palestinian flags), and after hours of
negotiations I was able to free them out.
The students however heard that hundreds of
students from other schools were detained and
so they decided on Wednesday morning to have
a sit-in in the town's mosque. This was the
same day that shops went on strike in Ramallah.
The students sent the military government of
Ramallah a petition asking for the release of
the detainees. After that, and around noon
time, the students dispersed. By that time, the
shops were re-opened in Ramallah, and it was
expected that the situation would be normal
the next day. In-fact I was relaxed enough to

go to Ramallah in the evening and have dinner there. On my return to Birzeit, I was told that the Military Governor called by phone, and when told that I was in Ramallah, he commented that I must be doing trouble there. This comment irritated me enough so that when he called again and summoned me to his office at 11:30 in the evening I did anticipate some trouble and hoped to convince him that his comment was unnecessary and that it was based on wrong information. Well, I had no chance to do that. I went to the Military Governor's office on schedule, but instead of meeting him, I was ushered into a guarded room where I waited for two hours before I got my first shock. At 1:30 in the morning an officer entered the room and told me that I was under arrest. He hand-cuffed and blind-folded me and placed me in a van which had the other deportees. We were then driven for seven hours towards an unknown destiny. During the trip we were very rudely treated and threatened with beatings whenever we attempted to utter a word. When the van stopped we were freed from the handcuffs and the blind-folds, we were told that this was the Lebanese border.

Our identity cards were confiscated and the deportation order was read to us. We were then told to move toward Lebanon and were warned that the crossing area would be later mined so that attempts of return would be seriously dangerous.

I believe that my deportation is an attempt to ruin one of the most enlightened cultural and educational centers in the West Bank. The College, which has been providing educational services to the community for the last 50 years had been closed last year for a period of three weeks. This was in the wake of demonstration that depicted the acts of deportation in

general and specifically, the deportation of
eight prominent members from Jerusalem and the
West Bank. The College is very well respected
by international organizations and has received
major financial contributions from them. It
stands for strong moral principles and engages
itself with purely academic and social issues.
It does not co-operate with the occupation
force in any manner and this might be the
over-all reason for the continuous harrassment
and intimidation that we were subjected to and
thatfinally resulted in the deportation of its
President.

Deportation of a citizen of an occupied
country – whether he is guilty or not – is
contrary to the accepted principles of the
international law. It is also a flagrant
violation of the Geneva Conventions of which
Israel is one of the signatories. It is
therefore extremely unfortunate that Israel
would resort to such actions against innocent
people. I do wish now to declare the illegality
of the Israeli action. I also wish to urge all
groups and individuals that involve
themselves with human rights to censure Israel
and urge it to make an immediate end to
deportation orders and to urge it also to
rescind its latest orders and allow us to go
back to our homes and families as soon as
possible.

Beirut, 27 November 1974

APPENDIX III

ISRAELI LIES AND HALF-TRUTHS, 16 JANUARY 1979

EMBASSY OF ISRAEL
WASHINGTON, D.C.

שגרירות ישראל
ושינגטון

January 16, 1979

Dear Correspondent:

I would like to acknowledge receipt of your recent letter concerning Birzeit University.

The facts concerning this institution are as follows:

1) Originally founded in 1924 as an elementary school, Birzeit University is a private institution. In 1930 secondary school classes were added, as were college-level classes in 1961. At the end of the 1965-1966 school year secondary-level studies were discontinued, and Birzeit continued to function as a college alone.

2) In 1972 the Birzeit administration requested permission to upgrade its academic status to university level and to issue Bachelor of Arts degrees. This was granted by the Israeli authorities in early 1973. Its student population has since doubled, to 600, with about 100 completing their studies each year. Most of the graduates to date have accepted teaching positions in Judea-Samaria and the Gaza District.

3) In recent years, Birzeit University has become a focal point of hostility and incitement against Israel. Among its board of trustees are a number of people known for their hostile public activity,

e.g. Mr. Hanna Nasser, who was expelled for such activity. Their presence at the head of the University provides a backing for the students to demonstrate and organize hostile and seditious public activity, which has received the support and backing of the PLO terrorist organisation. Such activity is illegal and has always been illegal in this area, and it is not surprising that the authorities have taken the necessary steps to bring the perpetrators to justice.

4) Nevertheless, the Israeli authorities have not interfered with the college's administrative development. Testimony to this is the fact that, last year, a large-scale expansion programme for the institution was authorized, as was an enlargement of its board of trustees.

5) Before 1967, the Jordanian Government refused to grant rights to any university institute in Judea-Samaria, and only with the permission of the Israeli Military Government was Birzeit established as an university degree-granting institute, with a planned expansion of 2,000 students, the creation of new facilities, addition of lecturers, the granting of higher degrees and the expansion of financial sources. Any study of the history of the institute will clearly show that only under the Israeli Military Government has the institute developed to the status of a free and independent academic institution.

6) Prior to the 1977–1978 academic year, a number of foreign lecturers found employment at the University. The condition for the granting of such permits, as in any state governed by law, are proper and legal entry to the country. A number of these lecturers, however, entered the country as tourists and their employment at Birzeit University without proper work permits was a violation of the law. Nevertheless, they have been allowed to stay and continue to teach until the end of the current academic year. With regard to the present 1978-1979 academic year, a list of thirty-two foreign lecturers was presented to the Military Government for the granting of such permits. All thirty-two were granted the permits.

7) There is not any censorship of study material. The single exception to this occurred in the case of a book by Mazal Rashid, which in fact, was permitted for use after examination. The only criteria used in such cases is the need to excise material considered to be seditious. In the current absence of higher education

regulations in Judea-Samaria, Birzeit is also free to use the
National Library of the Hebrew University and is not subject to
any customs duties, with regard to the importation of books.

I trust that these details will set this matter in Its correct
perspective.

yours,

Ariel Kerem
Information Dept.

APPENDIX IV

PRESS RELEASE FROM BZU AFTER 1979 CLOSURE

<u>STATEMENT FROM BIRZEIT UNIVERSITY</u>

Birzeit University has always been a free and independent academic institution since its founding in 1924 as an elementary school. In response to the needs of its community, the institution evolved naturally from secondary school to college and ultimately, although hindered by being under occupation, to a fully-accredited university. The University retains such status today, in spite of Israeli military occupation. Since 1967, however, our academic freedom has been thwarted and eroded by a series of arbitrary and harmful acts by the military authorities. The latest, a decision to forbid practice teaching by Birzeit University students in government schools, seriously disrupts our Education program and threatens the future of education in the West Bank and Gaza Strip.

For three years, Birzeit University students have carried on their necessary practice teaching in West Bank government schools under supervision of Israeli-approved teachers. No complaints of any kind were made against the students during this period. On the ninth of January 1979, Academic .Vice-President Dr. Gabi Baramki received a letter from the Education Supervisor in Ramallah informing him

of the decision of the Education Officer in
the Department of Education in Bethel to deny
approval for continued practice teaching this
year. No reason was given and, despite repeated
inquiries by Dr. Baramki, none has been
forthcoming to date. A letter of protest has,
therefore, been sent to UNESCO. Permission
for our graduate students in Education to
do research in the government schools has
similarly been withheld. (Both topics and
names of students have been submitted - see
Appendix).

Both the arbitrary nature of this decision
and the delay and disruption it causes in our
legitimate academic pursuits are typical of
the treatment accorded Birzeit University since
1967. Any study of this history reveals the
negative effects on this institution of
decisions made by the military government:

Illegal Customs Duties: Before 1967, Birzeit
University was exempt from customs duties under
Jordanian law. On October 8, 1970, a request
for continuation of custom-exempt status was
made. It was refused, contrary to international
agreements calling for the maintenance of the
status quo in occupied territories.

The amount paid in duty in the interim is
sufficient to have built a new building or
completely equip a laboratory (for example,
$46,000 in duty for laboratory and cafeteria
equipment only over twelve years). Construction
of our new campus has been rendered more
expensive as well. The duty on the steel for
the new Library Building alone amounted to
$20,000. Although, Birzeit University is not
subject to customs duties on books, it does pay
V.A.T. (12%). It is our understanding that
universities in Israel are refunded the V.A.T.
they pay; Birzeit is not.

Interference in Administrative Development: Two
years after a request was made for an
enlargement of Birzeit University's Board of
Trustees, permission was granted for a
reduction of its membership, from ten to eight
members.

Plans for a new campus site in Ramallah were
implemented in 1972, including municipal
expropriation of required land. After
architectural designs had been commissioned and
prepared and work was about to begin,
authorization was denied.

Work Permit Delays: Birzeit University applies
for work permits for its foreign lecturers
before they enter the country. In past
years, permits have been issued for varying
and arbitrary lengths of time; others have
been inexplicably delayed. For 78/79, 32
new applications were approved in principle,
although 11 have not yet been received.
Applications for 11 renewals have not been
approved to date.

Censorship of Study Materials: Despite claims
to the contrary, books and periodicals
ordered by Birzeit University are subject to
censorship. At least a dozen books have been
confiscated and not returned. The two latest
are a Bibliography of Palestinian-Jordanian
Authors from 1970 to 1975 and The Plays of
Ghassan Kanafani.

Vague and Hearsay "Charges": Repeatedly in the
Hebrew press and elsewhere, Birzeit University
is described in such terms as "a focal point
of hostility and incitement against Israel."
University officials are accused of providing
"backing for the students to demonstrate and
organize hostile and seditious public

activity." No one would deny the unpopularity of military occupation among the population of the West Bank and Gaza Strip, including the students of Birzeit University. It is libelous, however, to suggest that this institution encourages, fosters or backs illegal activities. For example, the regulations of the University require that classes proceed as scheduled during demonstrations.

Such charges and misrepresentations go beyond the delays and harassment that make up the usual climate under which Birzeit University operates. They are reminiscent of a similar slanderous campaign directed at Birzeit University in 1973, prior to its forced closing for two weeks and in 1974 when its President, Dr. Hanna Nasir, was deported.

We repeat that Birzeit University is a free and independent academic institution that pursues its legitimate activities in spite of arbitrary and harmful measures against it by the Israeli Military Government. We wonder, with some concern, how long we can continue in the face of negative decisions against us such as the forbidding of practice teaching by our students in government schools.

March 16, 1979

APPENDIX V

BZU PRESS RELEASE AFTER OPENING IN APRIL 1992

BIRZEIT UNIVERSITY
Public Relations Office

P.O. Box 14 BIRZEIT
-Phone 954381 Ramallah

21 April 1992/
For Immediate Release

PRESS RELEASE
BIRZEIT UNIVERSITY TO OPEN
Army Imposes "Gradual" Timetable After Over
Four Years of Closure

Ramallah — The head of the Israeli civil
administration in the West Bank, Colonel Gadi
Zohar, issued an order today reopening Birzeit
University after a closure of over four years. The
order opens the university in two stages, beginning
on 29 April when students from the faculties of
Science and Engineering are scheduled to return to
the new campus. The order came in the wake of a 19
April meeting between University administrators
and Israeli Defense Minister Moshe Arens and a
subsequent meeting between administrators and
military officials at Beit El military headquarters
near Ramallah.

During the meetings, University Vice-President
Dr. Gabi Baramki noted: "We stressed to the
Defense Minister that closing a university was
an unacceptable act of collective punishment. We

also affirmed the mission of Birzeit University
to provide quality education in a tradition of
democracy." University administrators also noted
that the closure of Birzeit University had been
unduly prolonged after an Israeli pledge to
re-open universities "gradually" in May 1990.

After receiving the closure order, Dr.
Baramki commented: "It is difficult to accept
that the last university allowed to re-open
is the one that is forced to re-open only
partially, despite the fact that the other five
universities have been functioning smoothly and
without incident. We told the Defense Minister
and other officials that it was difficult to
open a university in installments — we are a
whole academic community and our goal is to
remove tensions and impediments to learning,
rather than to re-inforce them by dividing
the student body. In this regard, we also
are concerned that all Gaza students who wish
to study at Birzeit or other universities be
allowed to do so freely and given whatever
permits are necessary." The order issued
to Birzeit University treated Gaza students
as "foreigners" and required them to have
residency permits to stay in the West Bank.

University spokesperson Albert Aghazarian noted
that during the years of closure, "education
itself was criminalized. We hope that education
will no longer be a criminal activity."
However, today's order ended with a threat to
close the university if "unsuitable activities"
take place, thus again raising the spectre
of collective punishment. Birzeit University,
extending its gratitude to the academics,
universities, governments and human rights
activists around the world who protested the
closure, also asks that friends of Palestinian
higher education remain on alert to protest any
further violations. -end-

APPENDIX VI

REPORT FROM FIVE HEBREW UNIVERSITY PROFESSORS ON ORDER 854-1980

Re Order 854

Report on the condition of Universities in the Occupied Territories

(1) Introduction

  A group of academic faculty members met on December 7, 1980, to hear a report and discuss the condition of universities in the Occupied Territories. In the course of the meeting the claim was made that the military government published a number of orders regulating the status of academic institutions in the Territories (order 854), and engaged in actions related to these institutions, in a way which injures academic freedom to a degree far exceeding that dictated by security considerations.

  Also under discussion were the negative reactions engendered in academic circles in Europe and the United States by those decrees and actions, and the lack of response to this issue by the Israeli academic community. At the end of the meeting the undersigned took upon themselves to work as a committee that would investigate all aspects of the problem and present their findings and recommendations to the Israeli academic community.

  The report is written so that the recommendations (part 4) are self explanatory; however, we recommend that this part be read in light of the detailed findings in the complete report.

(2) <u>Academic freedom and the military government</u>

One of the arguments brought up in the aforementioned meeting was that it is irrelevant to investigate infringements of academic freedom in territories under military government in which extensive security laws apply. There are, of course, restrictions which apply to all residents of the Territories - those this committee is not concerned with nor does it pass judgement upon them.

The committee's point of departure was that the security situation and the existence of a military government do not necessarily imply the abrogation of academic freedom, and that we, as members of the academic community have a particular status and sensitivity as regards this freedom. Therefore, the committee decided to confine its investigation to orders and procedures directed especially at the academic institutions which apply restrictions to them over and above those which apply to the general population. We refer to restrictions in the following spheres: appointment of faculty members; student admission procedures; the organization of curricular and research programs; selection of course material and the possession of suitable library and research material; finally - the ability to determine opening and closing dates of the institution. In addition we regard as an aspect of academic freedom and non-dependence the principle that academic recognition of an institution be made through academic considerations alone, and that an academic institution will not be required to be licensed by the administration.

(3) <u>The committee's mode of operation</u>

The committee held a series of meetings in order to clarify the points which we regarded as pertinent to an investigation. We would like hereby to express our thanks to the many people who gave of their time to meet with us. The committee met with persons who hold senior positions in the military government, or have done so in the past, in order to gather information about the academic institutions in the Territories, the background of the new legislation, and the integration of this legislation in the general policy of the administration. The committee met with two jurists from the Territories who

explained the legal regulation of educational
institutions in Jordan before 1967. We also met with
members of the administrations' faculty and with
student bodies of universities in the Territories,
and visited the universities of Bir Zeit and
Bethlehem. The findings of this report are based on
all of these.

(4) <u>Academic institutions in the Territories</u>
   Not every post-secondary institution is an academic
one. For the purpose of the committee's work an
"academic institution" was defined as that which
fulfills the two following conditions:
(a) the conclusion of a course of studies in the
institution enables the graduate to receive an
academic degree;
b) the degrees conferred by the institutions are
recognized degrees in the sense that they grant
generally accepted academic privileges, such as
the admission to advanced studies in other foreign
universities.
   Presently there are five institutions in the
Territories which confer recognized academic degrees,
or are working towards a stage in which recognized
degrees shall be granted. They are: Najah University
in Nablus, Bir Zeit University north of Ramallah,
Bethlehem University (administered by the Christian
order of Brothers - the Frere), the Islamic College
in Hebron, and the Religious College in Gaza. Among
those, Najah University has the largest number of
students and Bir Zeit University is the oldest,
although it only started conferring its own academic
degrees in 1973. Three of these five universities
(Najah, Bir Zeit and Gaza) are members in the
Association of Arab Universities, and one other
(Bethlehem University) has applied for admission to
this organization.
   In addition to academic institutions which deal
directly with education, there exist in many
countries institutions which guide academic education
and which also enjoy academic freedom. In Israel the
Higher Education Council is such an institution. In
the Territories a Higher Education Council was
established recently, and all the academic
institutions mentioned above voluntarily took upon
themselves to accept the authority of this Council,

which, inter alia, fixes the criteria according
to which institutions are granted recognition. The
chairman of the Council is Dr. Abed Al-Hak, the
President of Najah University. Officials of the
military government informed the committee that the
Council is directly controlled by the PLO and that
the military government does not regard it as a body
with which it can have contact. The committee saw no
point in dealing with this issue and decided not to
address the question of granting official status and
academic freedom to the Council, or the suggestion
that granting academic recognition to institutions
should be in this Council's jurisdiction.

(5) Preliminary Investigation
  A number of preliminary arguments arose in the
course of the committee's work, according to which
the issue of academic freedom is irrelevant as
regards academic institutions in the Territories. In
this part of our report we shall address these
arguments.
  The committee heard, especially from senior
military government sources, the claim that in the
Territories the academic cloak is merely camouflage.
The claim is that the academic activities are at
the best a guise for political activity and at
the worst a guise for subversive activity. This
claim is heard especially with regards to Bir Zeit
University. If this claim is true, then the question
of academic freedom simply does not hold. Therefore,
the committee started by addressing itself to the
following question: Do these academic institutions
maintain regular studies and/or research and do they
aim to grant their students orderly and up-to-date
education? The committee's findings in this area
are clear: In the universities which we visited,
academic activity is conducted according to accepted
norms and their administrations strive for the
advancement and regular maintenance of this activity.
  Even though there is some support for the view
that disruption in the conduct of studies, that
stems from friction with the military government,
may help a university in its public relations in
the Arab States, the committee's impression is that
the administrations made great efforts to assure the
regular execution of its curriculum, in spite of

their awkward position, "between the hammer and the anvil".

The committee rejects the preliminary claim that the true interest of academic institutions in the Territories is not academic at all. The committee does not have the ability or means to determine if, in addition to study and research, part of the university staff or students are connected to illegal activities. In any case, that is the task and function of the security forces who have at their disposal a wide range of security legislation. In the opinion of the committee, it is sufficient for our purposes to determine that in the academic institutions of the West Bank there exists a large population of students who are interested in acquiring a higher education, and a large number of lecturers who are concerned with providing that education. As stated previously, we have no doubt that this is so.

Another argument was put before the committee which also casts doubt on the nature of academic freedom in the universities of the Territories. According to this argument, the teaching in these universities (again, mostly at Bir Zeit) perverts reality and has little regard for the truth. When members of the committee requested evidence supporting this severe claim, they were told that in teaching geography of the Land of Israel maps are used on which Israeli settlements do not appear. The committee investigated this claim and found at Bir Zeit University maps published by the Survey Department of the State of Israel are used and that the course in geography of the Land of Israel includes a tour which lasts a number of days and covers many Israeli sites. There is no doubt that during the course in the geography of the Land of Israel there is also discussion of Israeli settlements which were erected in places on which previously Arab settlements stood. Obviously this fact may be presented in various ways. However, the committee found no evidence that the study of geography at Bir Zeit is based on denying facts.

With regard to Bethlehem University the charge is also made that the institution itself acts in a way inconsistent with academic freedom. It has been charged that the president of the institution was

relieved of his job only because he is not an Arab.
(The press even went as far as to say he was removed
because of a Jewish background.) The committee
investigated the claim in a frank discussion with
the outgoing president of Bethlehem University,
Brother Joseph Lowenstein. In that discussion (and
in others with members of the university), it
turned out that Bethlehem University applied to the
Jordanian government to grant official recognition
to the academic degrees conferred by the university.
The Jordan government replied that a condition for
such recognition was acceptance of the university by
the Association of Arab Universities. The university
knew in advance that one condition for acceptance as
a member of the Association was that it be headed
by an Arab. The university was thus forced to weigh
fulfillment of this condition against non-recognition
of the degrees it grants. At the recommendation of
the present president and after due consideration,
the decision was taken to appoint as president a
person who is an Arab with a suitable academic and
ecclesiastic background, while the present president
be given another high post in the university.
After hearing this, the committee concluded that
the decision of the university resulted from the
academic straits in which the university found
itself, and not from indifference towards academic
freedom in the institution.

In the committee's deliberations, a further charge
was raised concerning the involvement of the West
Bank universities in politics rather than academic
matters. According to this charge, the true purpose
of the West Bank universities is to develop cadres
of leaders and to build an intelligentsia that
will, when the time comes, serve the needs of
a Palestinian state. It is claimed that such an
objective exceeds the bounds of academic activity,
turning it into political activity. The committee
rejects such a charge, and declares that the
development of educated leaders who will serve the
community to which the university belongs is an
academic objective of the first importance. In this
matter the political desires in question are neither
here nor there.

(6) <u>The Relationship between the Military Government</u>
<u>and the Universities in the Territories</u>

Since the Six Day War, a complex network of
relations, positive and negative, has developed
between the military government and academic
institutions in the Territories. On the side of
positive cooperation, the most important fact is
simply that until the Six Day War there were no
academic institutions in the administered areas
while now there are five. Furthermore, the military
government itself approved the establishment of these
institutions. In the case of Bir Zeit University,
the military government approved its transformation
from a junior college (operating as an extension of
the American University of Beirut) to an independent
institution. The military government issued the
institutions with operating permits for specific
periods (although it is unclear on what basis it
was authorized to do so before Order 854, to be
discussed below) and allowed them to plan curricula
and instructional materials as they saw fit (within
the approved frameworks). It should also be noted
that the military government has allowed a number
of teachers from Arab countries (chiefly Jordan),
whose employment on the West Bank requires special
permits, to teach at the universities there. The
military government also recognizes the degrees
awarded by the universities (for the purpose of
salary increments for teachers, for example).

The establishment, continued administration and
development of the institutions required a certain
amount of necessary contact between the military
government and the universities. The committee gained
the impression that neither the military government
nor the universities were interested in cooperation
beyond the minimum called for. When we asked if the
military government requested any of the universities
to provide academic assistance (such as organizing
extension courses for local workers, various
laboratory services, etc.) the answer was negative.
For their part, the institutions appeal for
cooperation from the government only when the need
arises. This sometimes does arise when students need
practical apprenticeship in government institutions.
For instance, the military government was requested
to permit nursing students from Bethlehem University

to get practical training in government hospitals in the Territories and student teachers to practice-teach in government schools. Both requests were refused. Contact is also necessary when institutions apply for permission to conduct research requiring entrance and research on government institutions on the West Bank.

Thus, since the establishment of the institutions the reciprocal relations between them and the military government were limited for the most part to events of a negative sort in which the military government was engaged in a struggle with one or another of the universities, or vice versa. In addition, the military government as the sovereign authority in the Territories aimed to achieve legal regulation of academic activity in the Territories. To that end, it set up a committee which considered the problem for a considerable period.

The legal position of the universities was regulated, in the case of the West Bank, by means of Order 854, issued by the Command of Judea and Samaria on July 6, 1980. The committee knows of no analogous order pertaining to the Gaza Strip. Order 854 has wide ranging implications and its issuance was one reason for convening this committee. Therefore we are devoting a separate section to the order and the legal questions connected with it. (see #7 below)

According to the security legislation, the military government has wide powers which are sometimes exercised exclusively over academic institutions. The most notable and harsh example is the closing of a university, by instructing the administrator to order cessation of all teaching activities and research, and to prevent students and faculty members from entering the premises. (There is a difference between closing a university and closing off of the area in which a university is located.) Within the jurisdiction of the Judea and Samaria Command, there have been at least five closures of universities for varying periods, Bir Zeit University 'leading' with three closures, once (May 1979) for a period of more than two months. Closure of universities is a step taken, in almost every case, after serious disturbances on campus or around the campus in which students studying at that university were involved, and sometimes faculty members as well. There was one exception to this pattern: on November 13, 1980, Bir Zeit University was closed for a week after the military government blamed the university administration for delaying the cancellation of 'Palestine Week'. The military government's version was that the events were supposed to be called off the afternoon of the day on which the order was issued, while the university administration claimed that immediate cancellation of activities could not be carried out and that the activities in question were to be called off by evening of the same day. In any event, there is no disagreement over the fact that closing the university was intended as a punishment.

In other cases of closing a university, the military government justified its actions, both orally and in writing, in terms of punishing the institution for non-compliance with established norms. As mentioned, the procedure was used in most cases following serious incidents and disturbances, and there is no doubt that in those cases closure was not only in order to 'punish' but also in order to calm tempers and prevent repetition of those disturbances. But in most cases it is difficult to tell where prevention ends and punishment begins. It must be clearly stated that closing a university as punishment is simply an act of collective punishment and as such is unacceptable in principle. As for closing the university as a preventive measure, the committee's opinion is that the military government has more than sufficient means (including such stringent measures as bringing troops to the campus or imposing a curfew on the locale of the university) to prevent disturbances and the committee heard no convincing reason why, if the military government were prevented from closing the university, it would be hampered in any significant way from preventing disturbances of the peace.

Another point of friction between the military government and the universities concerns the government's treatment of requests for entry permits and work permits for teachers whom the universities recruit from outside the Territories.

There have been cases in which the military government has refused an entrance permit to someone

whom the university wished to employ as a faculty
member. Although it was not possible to investigate
each of these cases, the committee believes that
in these cases the military government has invoked
procedures applied to all requests for entry to
the Territories (in enforcing its visa policy)
and that it has not applied a policy exclusively
to the universities. In addition we view granting
universities in the Territories permission to employ
teachers from Arab countries as a positive step on
the part of the military government which supports
young universities which lack local teachers.
However, there have been a few cases in which
someone has been allowed entry to the Territories
and has been free to travel without restrictions
but has not been allowed to serve as a faculty
member. In these cases it is very difficult to argue
that the acts of the military government reflect a
general policy and not a policy aimed exclusively
at the universities. Moreover, if the government
allows someone to enter and move about freely, one
would infer that the government regards that person
as no danger to security. Preventing such a person
from joining the university staff can't be based on
security considerations and it involves unwarranted
interference by the military government in the
personnel policies of academic institutions. As
mentioned, the number of these cases is small. (The
committee learnt of three.)

In contrast, the problem exists of delays by the
military government in dealing with requests from
the universities concerning employment of faculty
from abroad. The administration must submit an
application for a work permit for every faculty
member who doesn't have a local identity card,
whether the person had a work permit in the past and
is already serving as an active faculty member, or
is someone the university wishes to employ for the
first time. In many cases, the military government
delays answering these requests for months, and
only after repeated written appeals. Thus sometimes
when the school year begins many faculty members
are still not sure of their legal status. Beyond
the question of proper administration, which our
committee doesn't consider itself authorized to

evaluate, such practices serve to sharpen resentments and bitterness, which could easily be avoided.

Another point of friction, where it is also difficult to know whether the delays constitute interference with academic freedom or a 'normal' result of administrative difficulties, concerns extending the framework of studies. At Bethlehem University, we were informed that the military government refused to allow the creation of additional departments beyond those that were permitted when the university was established. This forces the institution to broaden the scope of studies in a rather constrained way, or alternatively to give up its expansion entirely. In this category of complaints we include the complaint of the Trustees of Najah University in Nablus regarding a series of delays involving building permits for the new campus near Nablus. These delays limit and interfere with expansion of the university's program of studies. We didn't run into similar problems at Bir Zeit University which is now building its new campus at some distance from its old campus, which no longer meets the needs of a growing university,

It is axiomatic that academic activity can't take place without free access to books, journals and documents. Where security censorship exists (as in Israel) the objective is generally to prevent publication of material which can damage state security and not to prevent access to already-published materials. The military government maintains censorship which is aimed at this second objective; an order exists prohibiting distribution and possession of certain books. We were unable to obtain a list of these books from any official source, despite many requests. We were informed, however, by official sources that the list includes some 648 books nearly all printed in Arabic. The censor revises the list from time to time. The censor (or those authorized by him) are empowered to prevent the entry of banned books into the Territories by checking at border posts. On more than one occasion the military government has held up a bundle of books for checking and has then allowed through only approved books. In some cases the books which have not been approved are held at

border posts to be returned later to the seller.
In other cases attempts have been made to ease the
procedure by prior checking of lists, or checking the
books at the universities themselves before they are
catalogued. There have also been cases where the
disapproved books have disappeared and the addressee
has been unable to retrieve the purchase price, let
alone the VAT tax which has already been paid.

In connection with censorship of books, it appears
that the process has been evenly applied to the
whole population. The committee's view is, however,
that those chiefly affected are the academic
institutions. Even if, for the sake of argument, we
grant that there is justification in certain cases
for a policy of prohibiting the distribution and
possession of books, there is still room to demand
that the policies not apply to academic institutions.

The only instance known to the committee where
the military government carried out a "book search"
occurred at Kajah University in Nablus on February
11, 1981. (According to an official announcement by
the military government, the search uncovered
nothing.) Occasionally a search for 'prohibited
newspapers' takes place.

The argument in favor of prohibiting possession or
distribution of certain books is that these books may
be used as a means of incitement. Those who make the
claim ignore the fact that incitement is illegal, and
the moment a book is used for inciting, the person
who so uses the book can be charged with
transgressing the law. On the other hand, any book,
no matter how poisonous, is a source of legitimate
information for academic purposes, and more than once
poisonous books have served as documentary material
of value in academic research.

It is appropriate here to mention the question
of periodicals. There are newspapers, particularly
daily papers in Arabic (most of which are published
in East Jerusalem), whose distribution is prohibited
in the Territories. With regard to other Arabic-
language newspapers, the military government has
no official policy of prohibiting their entry into
the territories. Nevertheless, there is evidence of
the existence of an unofficial policy of repeated
delays and red tape wherever one of the universities
requests permission to bring books from an Arab

country to its library. Even after the military
government weeds out the banned journals from a
list submitted by the university, acquiring the non-
banned items has not been possible, because of this
unofficial policy.

Up to this point we have given details concerning
areas of conflict and mutual complaints between the
universities and the military government. As we
mentioned in our opening remarks, it is important
to stress that in at least three major areas of
academic activity – admission of students; setting
curricula and budgeting – the committee's impression
was that there has been no real friction between the
military government and the universities.

(a) Admission of Students

Although complaints of interference by the
authorities are heard, the committee's impression
was that in general the universities set the
standards for admission and act on them with no
outside interference. (One reservation is, of course,
that all students from outside the region must get
permission to enter the region.) To the best of
our knowledge, the only controversy between the
military government and the university arose when
the authorities expressed disapproval of benign
discrimination of candidates who had been imprisoned
or in administrative detention. Bir Zeit University
apparently permits those imprisoned for security
offenses or who were under administrative detention
to be admitted with a lower grade on the admissions
examination than other applicants. The reason given
the committee in justification of this policy was
that those who were imprisoned or detained were
adversely affected in their studies and academic
attainments. It is no surprise that the authorities
disapprove of this policy; nonetheless, it was our
impression that they acted with restraint in this
matter, and limited themselves to expressions of
protest.

(b) Setting the Curriculum

The universities in the Territories enjoy full
freedom in setting curricula (within the permitted
frameworks) and in selecting the material to be
included in courses. There have been no attempts
to cancel courses or restrict what is studied, and
this includes subjects which the authorities regard

as sensitive. The authorities limit access of the
universities to radioactive materials. However, the
committee does not view this as being motivated by
a desire to interfere in the course of studies,
but as a precaution resulting from the absence of
general procedures regarding use of an access to
such materials. While the universities, as mentioned,
enjoy full freedom to set courses of study, there
is evidence that military government personnel
have sometimes threatened to cancel or limit that
freedom. Such threats, if made, do damage even if
to all concerned there is no intention of acting on
them.

(c) Budgetary Policy

Although some of the funding sources for the
universities are certainly not to the liking of the
military government, it has so far shown no tendency
to interfere with the budget policy of these
institutions.

(7) The Legal Situation and Order 854
(7.1) The Situation in Jordan before 1967

In Jordanian law there is no general statute
governing the establishment and activity of
institutions of higher education. The only university
in Jordan in 1967 – the University of Amman –
was governed by a special statute. On the other
hand, Jordanian Law No. 16 of 1964 governs other
educational institutions, from kindergartens through
post-high school education institutions requiring
less than four years. That law states, among other
matters that:

1. private educational institutions require
permits from the Jordanian Ministry of
Education;

2. no one may be employed as a teacher,
whether in public or private institutions,
without a teaching permit from the Ministry
of Education; that permit is granted on the
basis of academic qualification and evaluation
of teaching ability. The Minister of Education
is empowered, on the basis of a recommendation
of the Committee for Educational Licensing to
cancel the teaching permit of a teacher if
convicted of a "moral crime".

3. teachers are forbidden to be members of

a political party or to take part in party
activities, whether inside the educational
institution or outside.
4. a special committee – the Supreme Committee
– supervises curricula and textbooks in
educational institutions. That committee
includes among its members, representatives of
the Ministry of Education, of the University of
Amman, of the liberal professions and education
experts.

(7.2) Developments after 1967
(a) Background
   Shortly after the Israeli forces entered the West
Bank, the powers of the Supreme Committee and the
Minister of Education were transferred to a military
government officer, called the "superviser", who
applied Law No. 16 to pre-university educational
institutions. {Since then, as described in the
general section of this report, several of the
post-high school institutions have developed into
institutions granting academic degrees that require
a four-year study period leading to a bachelor's
degree. That Law No. 16 was not meant to apply to
these institutions is clear: it states specifically
that it does not apply to the University of Amman,
the only university in Jordan when the law was
passed: and it provides that it applies only to
educational institutions in which the course of
studies is less than four years. Consequently,
universities in the Territories were governed by no
law at all.
   (b) Order 8S4
   1. Order # 854 issued by the Commander of the
region of Judea and Samaria, on July 6, 1980 is
composed of several parts:
   a. The Order extends the definition of
institutions regulated by Law # 16, so that the
law would apply to institutions of higher education
in which the period of study is four years or
more. This way the Order subordinates the academic
institutions to the control and the regulations
which apply to the other educational institutions.
The important implications of this subordination
are: (1) The need for a permit for the operation of
a private academic institution; (2) The need for a

permit to serve as academic staff; (3) Supervision
of curriculae and text-books in the academic
institutions.

   b. Concurrently with the extension of the
application of Law # 16, some essential amendments
were introduced to the law and to the regulations
issued according to it. (1) The full authority
of the Jordanian Education Ministry, concerning
licensing of private educational institutions has
been transferred to the supervising officer; (2)
The supervising officer was granted the authority
to annul, or refuse to grant, a permit to teach to
a person convicted of a violation of the security
legislation, or who was under administrative
detention; (3) Among the considerations entering
the deliberation over the granting of a permit to
a private educational institution, the supervising
officer can include "considerations of public order".

   c. The orders place restrictions on the competence
for the roles of director, teacher or student in
the educational institutions on the West Bank: (1)
An Israeli resident (including East Jerusalem) or
foreign resident, may not serve as director, teacher
or student in an educational institution, except by
individual permit certificate granted by a military
commander; (2) The resident of another administered
territory (Gaza, for example) entering the West Bank
may not serve as director, teacher or be a student,
except by special individual permit certificate
granted by a military commander.

2. Analysis

   It should be re-emphasized that part of these
orders change the legal situation of all educational
institutions and not just of academic institutions;
such are the restrictions on Israeli citizens,
foreigners and residents of other administered
territories; the ability to withdraw a teaching
permit or to deny it based on a conviction for a
security offence or an administrative detention; and
the possibility of using considerations of public
order in licensing private educational institutions.
To these must be added those innovations regarding
academic institutions which result from applying
Law No. 16 to them; the requirement for the
licensing of teachers by the supervising officer,

the supervision of curriculae and textbooks by the
said officer; prohibition of party membership and
of political activity by teachers. The restriction
on foreign residents and on residents of other
administered territories, though general, especially
hurts academic institutions. In the West Bank there
is insufficient man-power to shoulder the teaching
load in the universities, which are developing and
expanding rapidly, and the institutions attempt to
reinforce their academic staffs by outside visiting
lecturers. This is also true for students; it is
difficult to believe that the problem of students
from other administered territories will arise with
regard to pre-academic education.

It is important to emphasize one aspect of
Order 854: all changes introduced by it are
part of educational legislation and not security
legislation. It is generally agreed that amendments
to educational legislation should not give the
military government additional powers needed for
the preservation of security, but should provide
appropriate arrangements for the problem of the
educational institutions. Problems of security and
public order should be regulated by laws designed
for these purposes.

(7.3) Infringements on Academic Freedom due to Order
854
1. Infringements resulting from the application of
arrangements, appropriate to pre-academic education,
to universities
One of the basic characteristics of academic
freedom of universities is autonomy, protected by
law, in appointments and promotions of academic
staff, design of curriculae and choice of
educational material. Clearly this autonomy does
not imply a right to violate the general law.
But beyond the enforcement of the general law the
military government should not interfere with the
running of the institution (just as the institution
should not interfere with the academic activity of
its researchers). Such autonomy does not exist with
regards to non-academic educational institutions;
in their case it is accepted that it is necessary
to license teachers and maintain centralized
supervision of curriculae and teaching material.

This distinction between academic and non-academic
institutions is recognized both in the Israeli and
in the Jordanian law. Licensing academic staff,
licensing institutions of academic education, and
supervision of curriculae and teaching material are
alien to the idea of academic freedom. Restrictions
on party activity, beyond those existing in the
population at large (the situation in Jordan is
unclear), may be acceptable with regards to teachers
in the government school-system, who may be regarded
as public servants or state employees, but it is
clearly out of place with regards to academic staff
of private universities, which are supposed to
preserve their independence. We must stress once
again that the distinction between academic and
pre-academic institutions, and the insistence on
the independence of the former are recognized both
in the Jordanian Amman University law and in the
Israeli law on higher education. The "recognition"
of academic institutions is granted by a special
body, according to criteria different from those
pertaining to the recognition of lower educational
institutions. In the West Bank there is no such body
which has been granted recognition by the military
government. But, it is our view that the supervising
officer is not an adequate substitute.

2. Infringements resulting from the grafting of security aspects to general education legislation

According to the Jordanian Law #16 considerations
deemed pertinent for granting or annulment of a
teaching permit, or the granting of a permit to
a private educational institution, are related to
professional competence and to the suitability
of the person or the institution for educational
tasks. Granting the power to annul a teaching permit
because of a conviction for a security offence, or
because of an administrative detention, introduces
alien elements into the system of educational
considerations. The annulment of a teaching permit
under such circumstances is an additional punishment
of the teacher, over and above the punishment or
detention which were already meted to him, and
without demonstrating any connection between the
person's activity as a teacher and the conduct for
which he is being punished. It may be assumed that

said power shall not be exercised arbitrarily, and
that its exercise is subject to judicial review.
Nevertheless the committee is of the opinion that if
a teacher repeatedly violates the law, he should be
punished under the law, while his competence as a
teacher should not necessarily be affected. Annulment
of the permit of an educational institution (or
its shut-down because of disturbances) while the
institution is fulfilling its educational function
is a collective punishment for the teachers as
well as for the students, who are unable to study.
The lack of distinction between considerations of
professional-educational nature and those of public
order must not be part of the legal regulation of
the educational system.

3. Individual permits to persons who are not West
Bank residents
   Since permission is generally required, in order
to enter Judea and Samaria and to stay there,
such as for foreign residents, those restrictions
could have been used to restrict the movement of
teachers and potential students, without necessarily
infringing on academic freedom. But where the permit
requirement is imposed explicitly and specifically
only on teaching and study, (as it is on Israeli
residents and on residents of other administered
territories) it implies, with regards to academic
institutions, an infringement on their academic
freedom.

8. Recommendations
   The committee views the strengthening of the
tradition of academic freedom in the universities
of the Territories as an important step towards
peace in the region. The committee considers that
infringements on this freedom, due to security
considerations, should be reduced as much as
possible, and that such considerations should
not enter into legislation regulating academic
institutions. Hence we recommend that:
       1. Order 854 and all its appendices be
       rescinded.
       2. The military government and the universities
       should maintain contact so as to create a

condition that will ensure regular and peaceful
studies in the universities.
3. The issue of the legal regulation of the
universities in the West Bank be re-examined,
in consultation with educational personalities
in the West Bank and in Israel.
4. The military government should refrain from
closing universities.
5. The military government should reconsider
the abolition (or re-examination) of the list
of "forbidden books", and make it possible - in
practice — for universities to acquire books
and professional journals for their libraries.

1. Rescindment of Order 854 and its appendices
We have listed above the special restrictions
incurred by academic education due to the
application of regulations, appropriate to elementary
and secondary education, to universities. It is
important to note that so far the wide powers of the
military government under Order 854 have not been
exercised. The Order provided that existing operating
licenses would remain valid for a year and at the
end of the year, these licenses were automatically
extended for a further year. Although letters were
sent to the universities demanding information on
staff, students and curriculae, the Order has not
yet been invoked to interfere in these spheres. The
fact that the Order has not been exercised since
its promulgation strengthens our conclusion that it
was unneeded. We have stressed that Order 854 allows
for infringement of academic freedom and we heard no
convincing argument that this Order is a successful
solution to legal regulation of the universities. We
therefore recommend revokation of the Order.
    Concerning the restrictions on the movements
of teachers and students, and the requirement for
licensing "outside" teachers, we recommend that
restrictions imposed on higher education should
not go beyond those existing for the population at
large. Hence there is no need for special orders for
those who participate in higher education, and these
also should be rescinded.

2. Contact to ensure conditions for regular studies
    We were informed, both by representatives of

the military government and of the university administration of Bir Zeit University, that a "gentleman's agreement" was reached according to which the university authorities undertook to maintain order and prevent purely political activities on the campus, while the military government promised that if this undertaking was kept there would be no interference with the regular studies and the university would be allowed to operate without hindrance. Both sides expressed satisfaction with this arrangement, and were willing to base their future relationship on similar arrangements. The committee was particularly impressed by the fact that senior officials of the military government were willing to make such arrangements with the universities.

We feel that the goodwill of both sides should be exploited and arrangements clarifying the bounds of the educational institutions' undertakings and their responsibility for behaviour of students and teachers in the bounds of the institution, in order to provide an incentive for the university administration to supervise maintenance of order, on the one hand, and of the military government to respect the autonomy of the institutions, on the other.

In addition to agreement as regards operating the universities, such arrangements may improve relationships between the military government and the universities. This would also probably facilitate dealing with other problems such as providing visas for visiting staff without undue delay, and ordering books and equipment for university libraries and laboratories. Such arrangements would also facilitate enforcement of those censorship rules which shall remain in force, and the issuance of permits to extend programs of study, approve departments and building on university campuses.

3. Legal Regulation of the Universities

We have stated above that Order 854 is not a suitable legal framework for regulating the universities as it applies rules which were not meant for universities and are not suitable for them. We also reject the argument that there is

no need to revoke Order 854 as it is not fully
enforced.

We do not accept the argument (made both by
officials of the military government as well as
by members of the West Bank community) that the
universities must be regulated by law. Since 1973
the universities have existed and operated without a
legal framework, and it is difficult to see why the
necessity exists to regulate them. The supervision
required on security grounds can be exercised (as it
has been in the past) without resort to Order 854.

If the desire nevertheless exists to ensure a
proper legal framework for the universities, that
would allow for central academic control of the
opening and running of academic institutions, it
seems to us that the suitable framework should
be worked out in conjunction with the academic
community on the West Bank. The committee totally
rejects the argument that extension of Law No. 16
to cover the universities is the simplest method
of regulation, that ensures maximum continuity with
the Jordanian legislation which was in force on the
West Bank in 1967. This argument ignores the basic
differences between education at universities and
schools, which are our central concern, as members
of the academic community, as regards academic
freedom on the West Bank.

It should be noted that amongst the academic
community the definite preference was expressed
for maintenance of the position of non-regulation.
University people on the West Bank do not favour
the Jordanian model (which maintains royal licensing
and control of the universities) as a model worth
imitating. Some people even suggested that the best
arrangement would be one based on the Israeli model.
We were told that this suggestion was considered
by a special committee which advised the military
government, but that it was rejected in favour of
Order 854 and application of Law No. 16.

4. Closure of Universities

Closing a university by the military government
is an extreme and harsh measure which prevents
all members of faculty and students from studying,
teaching and doing research. This is also a
measure which receives the utmost attention and

severe criticism amongst the international academic
community.

One can distinguish between closing a university
as a punishment for an act by it or by some of
its students or teachers, and closing a university
as a preventive measure,, the object of which is
to maintain law and order. Closure as a punitive
measure is totally unacceptable as it is a form
of collective punishment which is imposed on all
students and teachers, with no connection to their
personal responsibility for the events which resulted
in punishment. According to the facts brought to
our attention this was at least the case regarding
the closing of Bir Zeit following the events of
"Palestine Week". The punitive nature of the closure
is obvious as the closure was only for one week,
with no indication that the situation would change
thereafter. In principle punishment should only be
imposed on offenders.

Even when closure is a preventive measure it is
not an acceptable procedure. We stated above that
in our mind the relations between the military
government and the universities should be based on
the understanding that the universities will be
responsible for order on campus. If the university
administrations will succeed in this, there will
be no need for further steps to ensure order on
campus. If they do not fully succeed in this, there
is no doubt that the military government has the
authority to enter the campus (like any other place)
in order to investigate and to deal with criminal
activities or breaches of the peace. There are
enough alternatives and less drastic ways of dealing
with the wide range of problems so that closure of
universities cannot be justified.

5. Books and Periodicals

There is no doubt that universities cannot exist
and run academic education without libraries which
will allow for access to books and periodicals.
One of the facets of academic freedom is that the
choice of materials and books is in the hands of
the academic staff of the institution. Members of
the academic staff, on their part, have a duty to
pursue the truth and to preserve a balanced view of
the materials taught. It follows that there should

be no restrictions whatsoever on the materials in
university libraries, for purposes of study, research
and analysis (though it is permissible, of course,
to limit the use which may be made of materials –
for incitement, for example).

We have seen that there are three ways in which
this central freedom is affected:

i) According to the security legislation a list of
banned books has been published. The ban applies to
West Bank residents, and not only to institutions of
higher education.

ii) All books ordered by the universities are
subject to examination by the censor who decides
whether to allow the institutions to keep them (we
were told, for example, that the censor tends to
disallow all books containing the name "Palestine",
and other books which are accessible to all –
including West Bank residents – in the National
Library of the Hebrew University).

iii) As regards professional periodicals the
barrier is administrative rather than legal: the
Bir Zeit librarian informed us that they have time
and again submitted a list of required Arabic
periodicals to the military government, but that
they never receive approval. We were given a copy
of this list and discovered that the vast majority
of the periodicals on the list are available in the
Hebrew University libraries.

As academics we object to all restrictions on
books, but in the framework of our present inquiry
we express no opinion about the general policy
on this matter. We merely ask that the military
government reconsider the ban, or at least try to
limit it as far as possible. Even if the general ban
is maintained we recommend allowing universities to
order a reasonable number of copies for an academic
library of any book. As far as periodicals are
concerned we recommend maintaining their existing
rule that no legal restriction be imposed on the
right to hold them in libraries. In order to
overcome administrative delays we recommend allowing
universities to order books and periodicals directly,
without prior approval of the military government.

Ruth Gavison (Law)
Yehoshua Kolodny (Geology)

David Kretchmer (Law)
Eliezar Rabinovitch (Physics)
Menahem Yaari (Economics)

This report was prepared by the above committee of
Hebrew University Professors, for an ad hoc faculty
meeting, called to discuss the issue. The committee
has prepared its report in Hebrew only.

APPENDIX VIIA

EXAMPLE OF REQUIRED LOYALTY OATH. A COMMITMENT FORM – 1982–3

<u>ISRAEL DEFENSE FORCES</u>
<u>CIVIL ADMINISTRATION FOR JUDEA AND SAMARIA</u>

<u>A Commitment for the Issuance of a Work Permit for the</u>
<u>Academic Year 1982/3</u>

Pursuant to my request for the issuance of a work permit for the academic year 1982–1983 which was submitted on _____ and without affecting my general commitment as per the request referred to above, I hereby declare that I am fully committed against indulging in any act and offering -any assistance to the organization called the PLO or any other terrorist organisation that is considered to be hostile to the State of Israel as indicated in the Act for the Prevention of Acts of Belligerence and Enemy Propaganda (Amendment No. 1) (Judea and Samaria No. 933; 5742-19S2, such acts being of a direct or indirect nature.

Date _____   Name of Applicant _____
                        I.D./Passport No. _____
                        Signature of Applicant _____

APPENDIX VIIB

WORK PERMIT A WITH ITEM 18, 1980

حيّز... ندى خا - سراسبي

המינהל האזרחי לאזור יהודה ושומרון
الادارة المدنية لمنطقة يهودا والسامرة

בקשה להיתר עיסוק
طلب اذن عمل

1. השם _____
   الاسم

2. הדת _____ 3. תאריך לידה _____
   الدين   تاريخ الميلاد

4. מקום הלידה _____ 5. הנתינות _____
   مكان الولادة   الجنسية

6. מס' דרכון - ת.ז. _____ 7. כפום הוצאתו _____
   رقم جواز السفر- هوية   مكان اصداره

8. סוג אשרת כניסה לאזור _____ 9. בתוקף עד _____
   درجة تأشيرة دخول المنطقة   صالحة لغاية

10. מקום מגורים באזור _____ טלפון _____
    مكان الاقامة في المنطقة   هاتف

11. כפום מגורים כחוץ לאזור _____
    مكان الاقامة خارج المنطقة

12. מקום מגורים לפני 1967 _____
    مكان الاقامة قبل ١٩٦٧

13. רמת ההשכלה _____ 14. ההתמחות _____
    الدرجة العلمية   التخصص

15. שם האוניברסיטה שסיים וכתובתה _____
    اسم الجامعة التي تخرج منها وعنوانها

16. המצב המשפחתי _____ שם הילד _____ הגיל _____
    الحالة العائلية   اسم الولد   العمر

    שם הילד _____ הגיל _____
    اسم الولد   العمر

17. נא לחת לי היתר-עיסוק כהחאא לצו כדבר איסיר על עיסוק יהודה ושומרון
    מס' 65 משנת 1967 - התשכ"ז
    ارجو منحي اذن عمل بموجب امر بشأن حظر العمل يهودا والسامرة (رقم ٦٥) من سنة ١٩٦٧

    ולהתיר לי לעיסוק בתפקיר _____
    وترخيصي العمل بوظيفة   في _____

    באתר/בהמרבנות. כיום _____ עד יום _____
    باجر/بتطوع من يم   الى يم

18. אני מאשר בזאת, כי קראתי והבנתי את התנאים שיחולו על קבלת היתר העיסוק.
    اصادق بهذا على اني قرأت وفهمت الشروط التي سوف نجبي عند استلام اذن العمل

תאריך _____   חתימה _____

APPENDIX VIIC

WORK PERMIT B WITHOUT ITEM 18, 1980

צבא הגנה לישראל
حيش , الدفاع الاسرائيلي

B-

המינהל האזרחי לאזור יהודה ושומרון
الادارة المدنية لمنطقة يهودا والسامرة

בקשה להיתר עיסוק
طلب اذن عمل

א

1. השם
الاسم _____

2. הדת
الدين _____ 3. תאריך לירה
تاريخ الميلاد _____

4. מקום הלידה
مكان الولادة _____ 5. הנתינות
الجنسية _____

6. מס' דרכון – ת.ז.
رقم جواز السفر- هوية _____ 7. מקום הוצאתו
مكان اصداره _____

8. סוג אשרת כניסה לאזור
درجة تأشيرة دخول المنطقة _____ 9. בתוקף עד
صالحة لغاية _____

10. מקום מגורים באזור
مكان الاقامة في المنطقة _____ טלפון
هاتف _____

11. מקום מגורים מחוץ לאזור
مكان الاقامة خارج المنطقة _____

12. מקום מגורים לפני 1967
مكان الاقامة قبل ١٩٦٧ _____

13. רמת ההשכלה
الدرجة العلمية _____ 14. ההתמחרת
التخصص, _____

15. שם האוניברסיטה שסיים וכתובתה
اسم الجامعة التي تخرج منها وعنوانها _____

16. המצב המשפחתי
الحالة العائلية _____

שם הילד اسم الولد	הגיל العمر
שם הילד اسم الولد	הגיל العمر

17. נא לתת לי היתר-עיסוק כהחאם לצו כדבר איסור על עיסוק יהודה ושומרון
מס' 65 משנת 1967 – התשכ"ז
ارجو منحي اذن عمل بموجب امر بشأن حظر العمل يهودا والسامرة (رقم ٦٥) من سنة ١٩٦٧

ולהחיר לי לעיסוק בחפקיד _____ ב
وترخيصي العمل بوظيفة _____ في

שכר/בהתנדבות. מירם _____ אלץ יצם
باجر/ بتبرع من يم _____ الى يم

תאריך _____ אחימה _____

APPENDIX VIII

LETTER TO SECRETARY BAKER, MARCH 1992

17 March 1992

Dear Secretary Baker,
We sincerely appreciate your efforts to bring
some sense of logic to this region. To this
end, you will be meeting today with Israeli
Defense Minister Moshe Arens. It is not yet
clear where our efforts will take us but, as
with an end to this obnoxious occupation, my
immediate concern is the re-opening of Birzeit
University.

A short drive north of Jerusalem there is a
modern campus with an 80,000 volume library,
science labs, auditoria and lecture theatres,
all barred to Palestinian students and
educators by military decree. This is Birzeit
University. Hanan Ashrawi is a professor of
English literature here. Dr. Haidar Abdal-Shafi
is on the Board of Trustees. In fact, Birzeit
University is home to more than half of the
Palestinian delegation to the Middle East peace
talks. And Birzeit University is closed by
Israeli military order.

The students and faculty — many of them
American trained — have refused to accept this
ban on education. Thus, while denied all the
proper facilities, over 2000 Birzeit students
are taking classes in the improvised atmosphere
of rented hotel rooms and offices, often within

sight of the padlocked campus. The situation is
Kafkaesque: Birzeit is closed, but make-shift
classes continue. And the erosion of quality
of education continues: off-campus classes are
matters of survival, they are no substitute for
an open university.

Since Madrid, we have had to face everything
but the establishment of confidence building
measures: from the takeover of houses in
Silwan and the revival of deportations of
Palestinians, to the building of settlements
and arming of Settler militias. All of this
in the name of "security". Meanwhile, since
May 1990, Israeli officials have declared
their "intention" to allow all Palestinian
universities to re-open. Even Israeli law
requires that the closure of an institution
last only for a "reasonable" period of time.
But there is nothing "reasonable" about an
unparalleled 52 months of university closure.
Despite repeated attempts, Israeli officials
have failed to portray the closure of Birzeit
as anything other than what it is: a crude
attack against an academic institution.

Over the years, the declared U.S. position on
the right to education and academic freedom has
been consistent. What is needed is the follow-
up. We expect you, Mr. Secretary, to stand
firmly behind your government's position and
confirm to Mr. Arens the seriousness with which
the U.S. views the continued use of military
closure against Palestinian educational and
cultural institutions. This criminalisation
of education cannot continue. The solution is
simple: open Birzeit University and put an end
the policy of university closure.

Sincerely,
G.A. Baramki, Vice-President.

INDEX

Lutheran church, Jerusalem, 89

Madrid peace talks, 1991,
131, 140, 162,
Mahshi, Khalil, 163
Majallet Ad-Drirasat a
Filisteeniyyah, 38
Mandela, Nelson, 113, 114
Mass in Time of War (Haydn),
159
Massachusetts Institute of
Technology, 163
Maurice, Captain, later Major,
Israeli military officer, 50,
51, 72
Middle East Council of
Churches, 92
military courts, establishment
in Occupied Territories, 55
Military Order 854, 93, 94,
95, 96, 149
military report from Hebrew
University professors, 182
Ministry of Education and
Higher Education, Palestine,
152–4
misinformation campaign,
against Birzeit University by
Israel, 49
Monroe, Elizabeth, 70
Moriah Hotel, Jerusalem, 122
Muthanna Ibnu Haritha, 12

Nabi Ya'coub (Neveh Yacov)
Hospital, 25
Nakba, 16, 76, 161
Nasir family, 5, 7, 10
Nasir, Aniseh, 11
Nasir, Hanna, 19, 34, 35, 36,
45, 46, 67, 68, 69, 70, 128
deportation, 50, 51–7, 65,
76, 169

return from exile, 141
Nasir, Kamal, poet, 22
Nasir, Mary, 8, 12
Nasir, Musa, founder of Birzeit
College, 17, 18, 19, 21, 34,
166
Nasir, Nabiha, principal, Birzeit
school, 10, 18
Nasir, Najla, 11
Nasir, Samia (married name
Khoury), 19
Nasir, Tania, 51, 52, 56, 141
Nasir, Wadi, 22, 23, 50
Nassar, Faruq Najib, 7
Nasser, Gamal Abdel, president
of Egypt, 22
Nasser, Kamal, poet, 43
Nazer, Dr Issam, 25, 29, 30
Nazzal, Darwish, 88
New Scientist, magazine, 19
New Yorker, magazine, 74
Newman, Cardinal John
Henry, 32, 33
non-violence, philosophy of,
113–15
non-violent protests
Birzeit University students, 45
Israeli army response to, 72
non-violent resistance
in face of closure, 81, 86
tree-planting as, 111
Nothomb, Simon-Pierre, 119
Notre Dame Centre, Jerusalem,
120
Nutting, Sir Anthony, 130

Odeh, Abdel Razzak, 53
Oslo Agreement, 1993, 129,
140–2, 152, 155

Palestine Horticultural Society,
9